Who is Racist?

Why Racism Matters

Who is Racist?
Why Racism Matters

Alexis Tan

cognella® | PRESS

For activists protesting racism everywhere: Change is coming.

Contents

Preface

As I write, thousands of Americans are demonstrating coast to coast to protest the death of George Floyd. Mr. Floyd, a Black man described by family as a gentle giant, died while a White police officer had his knee on Mr. Floyd's neck for almost 9 minutes, including 3 minutes after he was not responsive. Mr. Floyd was lying prone on the sidewalk, handcuffed behind his back, and was not resisting. He pleaded several times, "Please, I can't breathe," and at one point called for his mother. The police officer who did not release his knee even after Mr. Floyd lay motionless on the sidewalk was arrested, booked, and charged with second-degree murder. Mr. Floyd's killing was one of several deaths of Black men and women in the past several years at the hands of police or, in at least one case, White vigilantes. Rage and pain showed in the faces of demonstrators, Black, Brown, White, men, women, mostly young. Some invoked Martin Luther King Jr., who, while advocating nonviolence said in a speech at Stanford, "A riot is the language of the unheard." A "Justice for George Floyd" petition on Change.org started by a 15-year old generated more than 6.3 million signatures in 24 hours at the rate of one signature every 2 seconds, the fastest growing petition ever in Change.org. Nike posted on its Instagram account, which reaches 112 million followers, the following:

> For once, Don't Do It: Don't pretend there's not
> a problem in America. Don't turn your back on

racism. Don't accept innocent lives being taken from us. Don't make any more excuses. Don't think this doesn't affect you. Don't sit back and be silent. Don't think you can't be part of the change. Let's all be part of the change.[1]

In response to protests, some turning violent, the president of the United States exhorted governors to use force and the military to confront the protesters, threatening to unleash "vicious dogs" and "ominous weapons" on those who breached the White House wall and 10-year prison sentences for protesters who were arrested.[2] The president's presumed opponent in the November elections called for empathy, compassion, and healing. Representative and civil rights icon John Lewis denounced the violence and looting and urged protesters to organize, demonstrate, sit-in, stand up, vote. Former president Barack Obama urged a new generation of young activists to "sustain momentum to bring about real change" by voting and participating in politics. A line of almost all White women formed between police officers and Black protesters in Louisville, posting "This is what you do with your privilege." A number of law enforcement officers in several cities knelt and marched in solidarity with protesters while others threw tear gas cannisters at peaceful crowds.[3] As I write tonight, these are the words and images in my mind.

I wrote most of this book before George Floyd's death. Most of America is angry, disgusted, frustrated, and grieving. My commentary on racism and many of the examples I use to demonstrate racism seem now to be tepid academic exercises from an ivory tower that do not capture the seriousness of the problem. Racism is a public health hazard in America. People of color are victimized every day. So are poor people, people without power. Innocent Black men and women are being killed with alarming frequency. If there is a silver lining, most Americans of every color want to do something about it. But how do you change a system? How do you change a culture? How do you reverse a history of exploitation? Change, a university president I admire once told me, "begins with each one us." So, it's up to us to confront racism, understand what it is, and control it in our personal and professional lives.

If you are like most people, race is not among your favorite topics. We don't like to talk about how some police officers might be racist; how some of our government officials, doctors, teachers, judges, journalists, neighbors, the media, the American political and economic systems might be racist. We don't like to talk about how Black, White, and Brown people may be different from each other, or how we like some people better than others because of their skin color. We don't talk about race because it makes us uncomfortable. What is the right thing to say so we don't appear to favor one race over another? Or worse, so we don't appear to be racist? So, we keep quiet, avoid or change the topic, talk about how we are coping with the Coronavirus pandemic and our plans for next year. When the topic comes up, we say, "Race is not my problem." Or, if we agree that racism is everyone's problem, we may become frustrated because we are at a loss when asked what we can do about it, so we stop talking.

But some of us don't have a choice. People of color are victims every day, such as the mother who fears for her teenage son when he goes jogging in a park. Research tells us that Black Americans talk about race more often to their children than White Americans, to prepare their children for a racist world. I talk about race to my graduate and undergraduate college students at a large public university where I am a professor. I teach a course called "Communication, Stereotypes and Prejudice" and do academic research on why most people are unconsciously biased and how these biases can be controlled. My teaching and research have been shaped by personal experiences with prejudice and by my academic training at the University of Wisconsin-Madison where I was introduced to civil rights activism, volumes of research on the origins and consequences of racism, and the professors who did the research. So, you might say that I was programmed to do my work and, in a more specific sense, to write this book.

Fueling my work and trying to remain objective have been experiences and observations demonstrating that race indeed matters at a personal level and, more importantly, in American culture and society: People are treated and evaluated differently because of the color of their skin. This realization—that skin color matters—has roots in my childhood in the Philippines, a former colony of the United States, and was later reinforced by experiences and observations as an immigrant in the United States.

My attempts at understanding and providing coherence to these experiences have largely been limited to journal articles and textbooks I have authored, filled with data and charts, reaching primarily other academics and students. This book is an attempt to reach you, a larger audience. I hope to show how race indeed matters, and why racism affects all of us, and, more importantly, how we can each do our share to control racism.

The time is now to talk about race. Race relations in the United States have deteriorated in the past 4 years, while violent hate crimes have increased. Large majorities of Americans say racism remains a major problem[4] and that race relations have deteriorated since President Barack Obama's election.[5] Violent crimes motivated by hate and directed at racial and ethnic minorities, particularly Hispanics and other minority groups, based on gender identity and disability reached a 16-year high in 2018.[6] Why this disturbing trend? Most Americans (65%) believe it's more acceptable today to express racist views, and 45% say racism is more acceptable.[7] According to the majority of Americans (56%), President Donald Trump is contributing to the problem by making race relations "worse."[8] Whether this is a fair assessment can be informed by recent scientific research about how racist acts are activated. I tell you about this research in this book, along with recent advances in our understanding of the consequences of racism, and, on an optimistic note, how racism can be controlled.

I revised this preface after George Floyd's death. For sure, events still to unfold will alter the narrative. But, the basic premise of this book remains: Race matters.

Acknowledgments

To my family, for sharing your stories, thank you.

Introduction
Why Talk About Race?

Many of us see racism as the other person's problem because we are not racist. Unless we are victims, racism is what we read about in newspapers or see in nightly television news, not a reality we have to face day to day. But racism is a problem for all of us. Large majorities of Americans believe that racism is a major problem in American society. Some White supremacists have called for a "race war." News and social media posts are filled with stories about racist acts: a Black man shot to death by vigilantes while jogging, police being called by racists to investigate people of color engaged in lawful everyday activities in personal and public spaces. Is the immigration question about race? Are government policies and statements by the president and other government officials regarding the COVID-19 pandemic based on race? Most people, and some journalists, are reluctant to call racist acts racist, prompting the Associated Press to recommend that "journalists call it what it is; do not use "racially charged" or similar terms as euphemism for racist or racism when the latter terms are truly applicable."[1] Science can help us understand racism. So can stories from the frontlines. Considering the increase in recent years of racist hate crimes and incidents, there is some urgency for people like you and me to take responsibility for mitigating the problem. And the first step is talking about racism and understanding the nature of the beast.

Although most Americans say that racism is a major problem, and that relations between the races are worsening,[2] not surprisingly, few Americans actually believe they are racist. According to a CNN poll, only 13% of White Americans admit to being racially biased, but 43% say they know someone they consider to be racist.[3] It's not acceptable to be racist in American society. If we believe in the U.S. constitution and a professed value of equality for all, then we can't be racist. Consider a Nevada rancher who was involved in a dispute with the government over grazing rights on federal land. In an interview with the *New York Times*, he referred to Black Americans as "the Negro" and wondered if they were "better off as slaves" than "under government subsidy." He recalled driving past homes in Las Vegas and seeing Black people who "didn't have nothing to do." At a news conference after the *Times* interview, he repeated the same sentiment, asking, "Are they slaves to charities and government subsidized homes? And are they slaves when their daughters are having abortions and their sons are in prison?" After the interview, the Associated Press reported that the rancher's official Facebook page said that he was a "good man, he loves all people, he is not a racist man."[4]

The rancher's racist statements and his denial of being a racist can be explained in at least two ways. He is not a racist, does not think that Blacks are inferior members of American society, and was simply commenting on an observation. Or, he has racial biases that he does not admit to or is not aware of.

Recent research on racism suggests that the second explanation is more plausible. Over 80% of Americans—White, Black, Brown—have racial biases they may not even be aware of. Because these unconscious biases are uncovered in voluntary tests (the Implicit Association Test), the percentage in the general population may even be higher. People who take the Implicit Association Test are typically more educated, have access to a computer and the internet, and want to understand their biases.[5] The good news is that most of us with unconscious biases (I am among the 80%) want to control those biases so that biases don't control our evaluations of and behaviors toward members of other racial groups.

Racism is demonstrated more often in subconscious acts—language, evaluations, interpersonal interactions—than in violence and aggression, or hate crimes. The distinction is in the severity of consequences for the victim. While subconscious racism, sometimes called microaggressions, often results in severe psychological and emotional stress and evaluations that can cause economic loss, inferior health care, unfair treatment in the criminal justice system and racial profiling, hate crimes often result in physical injury or death. Hate crimes are committed by unapologetic racists (see Chapter 3), who are, fortunately, by some estimates, no more than 10% of Americans.[6] Recent history shows that hate crimes are still, or even more so today, a part of everyday life in America and therefore should not be ignored or cast aside as aberrations in an otherwise egalitarian society. As a reminder that haters are out there, I tell you stories about violent racist crimes. But I also tell stories about subconscious acts of racism that are more common than violent hate crimes. These acts are subconscious because we automatically engage in them without thinking. Some of these stories you may have heard before because they were reported in the news, and other stories you may be reading for the first time because they are based on my personal experiences and the experiences of friends. I have dramatized some of the stories to make a point. All are based on true incidents.

My first story, an account of a hate crime, is based on a true incident reported in the local newspaper of Coeur d'Alene, Idaho, where Katherine (my wife, not her real name), Lakota, our long-haired German Shepherd, and I have a vacation home. You may have heard of Coeur d'Alene and the adjoining town of Hayden Lake. Coeur d'Alene is a lake city often identified by travel magazines as one of the top 10 undiscovered tourist attractions in the United States, known for its lakes, rivers, mountains, and golf courses. Some years in April, you can golf and parasail over the lake in the morning and alpine ski in the afternoon. Coeur d' Alene and adjoining Hayden Lake have been identified by White supremacists as favored "homelands" because almost all of the population is White. Hayden Lake is the former headquarters of the Aryan Nations. Imagine Katherine (who no one would mistake for a woman of color) and I, a biracial couple in what was at one time the epicenter of White supremacist groups from all over the United States. We stubbornly chose to buy a cabin there because we did not want a small group of racists to prevent us from realizing a dream, an idyllic place by the water our families could enjoy, and just a 2-hour drive from home. And so, we settled in, uneasy at first, but gradually feeling more comfortable. I used to play a mental game by guessing whether each White person I saw was a racist. Most of the time, I concluded that folks in dirty pick-up trucks with gun racks were racists—until one of them pulled my vehicle out of a snowbank in January. So, after a while, I gave up my guessing game. I was no better than the racists themselves—judging people by the way they looked and the vehicles they drove. To their credit, the people of Hayden Lake and Coeur d'Alene, with help from the Southern Poverty Law Center, drove the Aryans away and have turned their former headquarters into a peace park. A handful of White supremacists—count them with fingers in both hands—are still active, hanging nooses on the doors of the headquarters of the Human Rights Commission, painting swastikas and racial slurs on fences and doors of private residences owned by racial minorities and biracial couples, depositing hate leaflets in people's yards, and picketing Mexican food stands with signs that say "Honk if you want Idaho White." During peaceful citizen protests of the killing of George Floyd, small bands of men and women armed with semiautomatic weapons and other guns patrolled downtown Coeur d'Alene. They said they were protecting protesters and businesses from an expected invasion by leftist groups (Antifa). This rumor proved to be false, spread on the internet by hate groups.

My experiences as a person of color in overwhelmingly White (and Republican) Coeur d'Alene and Hayden Lake have mostly been pleasant. Along with Katherine, I have felt welcome in public places, retail establishments, banks, restaurants, government offices, the corner gas station, WalMart. Is it because I am no longer the young pony-tailed Polynesian or Asian angry young man? Is it because people were trying to dispel the stereotype of their town? But most of the time, I am still uneasy and cautious. The haters are still out there.

It is in Coeur d'Alene where Jose Garcia is raking leaves in the yard of his modest farm house. Parked in his driveway is his van equipped with a pull-out stand: "Mexican tacos," says a big sign in red painted on the side of the van. Jose Garcia looks up from the pile of leaves he is raking as a white pick-up truck, front hood caked in mud, a Confederate flag painted on a door panel, roars by the street in front of his house, disappearing in a cloud of dust. A few seconds later, the truck reappears, this time going slower. A White man with a shaved head and a Nazi cross tattoo on his left arm leans out of the driver's window, gives Jose the finger, points to the rifle in the gun rack behind him, and yells, "Dirty Mexican, go home!" The truck makes a U-turn and drives by the house again; this time both the driver and passenger are yelling even louder. Jose tells his wife and children to get in the house. The men park the truck. They get out and walk toward Jose. One of them is holding the rifle. Jose runs to his van and retrieves a kitchen knife, which he hides in his shirt and dials 911. Police officers respond and arrest the two men, who were later charged with hate crimes. The men were acquitted by juries twice, their defense attorney claiming, "It's not about race." On the third try, a persistent district attorney obtained a conviction on related charges. The men were sentenced to several years in prison. After the conviction, a handful of picketers (10 at most), marched by Jose's taco truck with signs saying, "Honk if you want Idaho White." By most accounts, hardly anyone honked. And the good people of Coeur d'Alene lined up for tacos at Jose's stand.

Jose Garcia's story reminds me that racism happens to ordinary people simply because they look "different," have a different skin color. And personal consequences are often not captured by a headline and news clip unless a victim is killed. I can imagine the constant fear in his children and wife that someone else will come after them.

Jose's story also reminds me of my own racism, unconscious for sure, directed not at people of color but at White racists. As I read back this story, I find that my dramatized narrative, although based on a true incident, is filled with preconceptions or stereotypes of the bad guys and even the good guy. The truck passenger is bald with tattoos (like all racists). The vehicle is a pick-up truck with a gun rack; it's not a BMW X5 or a Honda Ridge Line. The truck is dirty, probably from hauling ATVs to a muddy river basin where the drivers fire their guns in target practice, see who can drive their ATVs the fastest in the mud, and leave their trash behind. Jose has a portable taco stand. His house sits by an unpaved and dusty road, not on Hayden Lake Country Club Lane. And he arms himself with a kitchen knife when confronted by the racists.

In my attempt to inject some drama, I succumbed to my unconscious biases, drawing a caricature of racists who unfairly put them in a visible category of White people who may not be racists. Many folks drive old, beat up pick-up trucks because that is what they can afford. Some trucks may be dirty because the owners work in construction sites or ranches. Gun racks are common in states where people hunt game for food. Bald heads and tattoos? Take a look everywhere. My portrait of Jose is no less stereotypical. He has a small house by a dirt road, four children, and a taco stand. And he uses the first available weapon for self-defense, a knife.

In reality, racists and their victims come from all spectrums of American society. A well-known supporter of the Aryan nations in Coeur d'Alene was an attorney who drove a Cadillac Escalade. Some of the strongest supporters of racist public policies are some of our elected officials. And some racial minorities in Coeur d'Alene and Hayden Lake own multimillion-dollar waterfront homes.

Who is a racist? Clearly, the 10% of Americans who openly proclaim their hate and their membership in hate groups demonstrate their racism by their actions. Many have been tried and convicted for their hate crimes. They can be identified: Hitler, the Ku Klux Klan, neo-Nazis, White supremacists. If you are interested, the FBI, the Southern Poverty Law Center, and the Anti-Defamation League keep track of hate groups in the United States.[7] More difficult to recognize are the 80% of Americans whose racist actions are activated by unconscious biases. Some in this group defend their actions by invoking a higher authority—an employer, religion, the "law," or the U.S. Constitution—denying any personal responsibility. Most in the 80% (like myself) admit to and work to control their unconscious biases, including many physicians, teachers, lawyers, judges, law enforcement officers, journalists, and everyday folks. To talk about race, we have to talk about the range of racism, from violent acts to everyday microaggressions, to hateful language. Racism is language, symbols, and actions. Here are some examples.

Violent Racism

In February 2020, Ahmaud Arbery, a young Black man, was chased by two White men while he was jogging. One of the men shot and killed him. In May 2020, George Floyd, a Black man, pleaded "I can't breathe" while a White Minneapolis police officer knelt on his neck for almost 9 minutes. Mr. Floyd was handcuffed, prone on the sidewalk. He was later pronounced dead at the scene. The mayor is enraged. The police officer who killed Mr. Floyd has been charged with second-degree murder. Hundreds of thousands across the United States and in some foreign capitals have been protesting after Mr. Floyd's death, calling for an end to racism and demanding change.[8]

In 1955, Emmett Till was 14 years old when he was abducted from his aunt's home in Mississippi by two White men, beaten, mutilated, shot in the head, and dumped in a river. Emmett had been accused by the wife of one of the killers of whistling at her while he and his friends were paying for bubble gum they had bought in her store, a charge the woman said many years later was not true. The men responsible for the murder were found innocent by an all-White jury after less than an hour of deliberations. Emmett's mother insisted on an open casket at his wake. The brutality of his murder became a rallying cry for civil rights activists. In 1956, Emmett's killers admitted to the crime in a story they sold to *Look* magazine for $4,000. Several memorials were erected to remember Emmett, among them one in Graball's Landing in Mississippi close to the river where his body was found. The memorial had been repeatedly vandalized, riddled with bullet holes, stolen, and dumped in the river, and it had to be replaced at least four times. In 2018, two White college students posed with their rifles in front of the memorial and posted the photo on Facebook. In 2019, a new 500-pound bulletproof memorial with protective glass and reinforced steel was dedicated, the fourth to be erected at the site. The new memorial was built by the Lite Brite Neon Studio in Brooklyn, New York.[9]

As I read about Emmitt Till, I wondered, "Why the hatred? The irrational sensitivity regarding any alleged interaction between Black males (a child!) and White women? Why this evil, condoned by the 'justice' system?"

Institutional Racism

It is spring 1966. Three young Filipino graduate students set out from Madison, Wisconsin, for Fort Lauderdale, Florida, the place to be for spring break, they had heard. Somewhere in Mississippi, they stop for dinner at a roadside café advertising chicken fried steak for $2.99. They park their 1962 Oldsmobile F-85 with a hole in the floor covered with a piece of plywood and walk into the restaurant. Inside are a dozen tables covered with vinyl, bottles of ketchup, and salt and pepper shakers on top. Pinned on one wall is a Confederate flag. Half of the tables are occupied. The Filipinos stand by the cash register at the entrance, unsure of whether to find a table or wait to be seated. One says to the others, in Tagalog, "We probably should leave," noting that all the people seated at the tables are White. One, two, five minutes pass; the young men are nervous and restless. A few people glance up at them, faces expressionless, as if they are invisible. The Filipinos are about to seat themselves at an empty table (they are hungry, and $2.99 was appealing) when a young woman approaches them, a smile on her pretty White face, and asks if they want dinner. "Follow me," she says, and leads them through the kitchen to a back room with three tables. Seated at one of the tables are a Black couple with two young children. One of the Filipinos tells the waitress, "We would rather sit out there in front." She looks genuinely embarrassed, her face blushing, and says, "It's much better for you here. Those tables are reserved." What to do, the young men wonder. Images of Rosa Parks flash through one man's mind. The other two are already seated at the table. "This is fine; we're hungry, no big deal," they tell their friend. After finishing the chicken fried steak (delicious) and leaving a generous tip for the waitress, the Filipinos walk back to their car. There are still a few people in the main dining room. Most of the tables are empty. No one pays the Filipinos any attention. They are invisible.

As I wrote about this experience, I thought the waitress was not to blame. How do you fight a system? Was my anger at the White patrons of the restaurant justified?

In another country, decades later, I am in Johannesburg, South Africa, 2 years before apartheid is dismantled. Nelson Mandela is still in prison. Katherine (my wife, not her real name) and I are having dinner in the home of a university professor and his wife, an artist. We are sitting in an outdoor patio shaded by grape vines on trellises and fig trees, beside a swimming pool. We are being served by Black women, "staff people," our host tells us. I had been invited by our host's university to give a lecture about my research on racial prejudice. Our hosts are "English;" their descendants had come to South Africa after the "Afrikaaners," who had come from the Netherlands. I knew that under apartheid any kind of relations, especially intimate relations, between Whites (Afrikaaners and English) and non-Whites was prohibited and punishable by imprisonment. The person of color was the one often imprisoned while the White person got off with a warning or a fine. So, I asked my host what my racial classification would be and whether I was at risk of imprisonment for sharing the same hotel room with Katherine who was clearly not a person of color. Visibly embarrassed, our hosts explained that as a visiting "dignitary," I was considered to be an honorary White and there was nothing to worry about. His wife then apologized for apartheid and said that it would die when Mr. Mandela is released. "About time," her husband said. Besides being immoral, apartheid made no sense, he continued. "Did you know," he told us, "that Chinese South Africans are classified as colored or Black depending on their skin pigmentation, while Japanese South Africans are White, regardless of their skin color?" "And," he said, "that's because the government wishes to access Japanese capital and technology."

Did I make the right decision, accepting my "honorary White" designation? Or should I have insisted on staying with my wife in a hotel room as an Asian/Pacific Islander and risk imprisonment? For an incisive and personal account of growing up biracial in apartheid South Africa, I recommend Trevor Noah's *Born a Crime*.[10]

Religion as an Excuse

In September 2019, the owner of a resort in Mississippi often used for weddings told a biracial couple (the groom is Black, the bride is White) that they were not welcome. The owner said, "First of all we don't do gay weddings or mixed race because of our Christian race, I mean our Christian belief." A video of the interaction attracted more than 2 million viewers across Twitter and YouTube. Critics called the venue owners "hateful racists" and called for the business to be closed. The owner then issued an apology, saying, "My intent was never racism, but to stand firm on what I assumed was right concerning marriage," and acknowledged that biracial relationships were never mentioned in the Bible.[11]

Reading this news report, I wondered how many racists who get so riled up by interracial couples actually read the Bible and whether their rage is fueled by something else. Looking back at my own experiences, I reluctantly conclude that this rage, shown by some White men (not *all* White men, but by some who are racist) and more likely directed at men of color in interracial relationships, is grounded on several myths. One is that men of color, particularly Black men, are hypersexual and are out to "steal" White women.

And second, mixing of the races is an existential threat to the purity of the White race. Of course, these myths are held by a very small proportion of White Americans, and similar beliefs can be found across the world: Men from outside of a society's mainstream "race" are perceived to be threats to racial purity. I reluctantly offer this explanation because this question is almost impossible to study scientifically. Most people will either not talk about the issue or will lie about their true feelings. And causality cannot be proven. I cannot study the problem in a laboratory. So, take my explanation cautiously, with, as they say, a grain of salt. For my part, I have been a target of this anger.

In the mid-70s, Katherine and I visited good friends in a small town in North Dakota where the husband was a veterinarian. Philip (not his real name) is Filipino; Susan (not her real name), his wife of 12 years, was born and raised in New England, spending summers at her family's Hamptons vacation home. Susan, like Katherine, is not a person of color. The four of us went to a bar downtown after having dinner at the Ramada Inn restaurant. We ordered drinks; a small band was playing country western music. We sat at the table enjoying our drinks. After about 15 minutes, a waitress approaches our table and tells us she has a message from the men (yes, they were White, cowboy hats and boots) at the next table. She hands me a table napkin with a message scrawled: "LEAVE NOW; and leave the women behind"). I looked up at the men, who were staring and glaring at our group. One of them says, loud enough to be heard over the band's music, "GO BACK TO THE RESERVATION. And LEAVE THEM WITH US." What to do? Call the police? (I should trust them, but do I really? What was the infraction?) Confront the men? There were four of them. We leave without saying a word and spend the rest of the evening at the casino on the reservation.

This dramatized incident and others like it have made me extra careful about where Katherine and I go to have a drink and dinner or enjoy a band. We avoid any place that I prejudge to be a hangout of racists. Then I have to remind myself that this is bias, almost just as bad as the racism I abhor. Most cowboys are good people. Anyway, first chance I get back home, I enrolled in a Tae Kwon Do class. That was good for my soul.

My Freedom as an Excuse

In 2013, a man identified by the Southern Poverty law Center as a hard-core White supremacist and anti-Semite bought large tracts of land in a small North Dakota ghost town. He sold lots to other White supremacists. In a supremacist message board, he wrote, "For starters, we could declare Mexican illegal invaders and Israeli Mossad/IDF spies no-go zone. If leftist journalists or antis come and try to make trouble, they just might break one of our local ordinances and would have to be arrested by our own constable. See?" The man added that he hoped residents of his enclave would fly at least one "racialized" banner such as a Nazi flag.[12]

Reading this news report, I wondered who this person was. What motivated him? (Some of the answers I found are discussed in Chapter 3.) But I was also struck by another news report about him.

The *Los Angeles Times* reported in November 2013, that our White supremacist found out during a taping of Trisha Goddard's talk show that he is part Black. He had submitted DNA for testing, and the results revealed during the taping of the show that he was 86% European and 14% sub-Saharan African. As the audience cheered and laughed, the man protested, "Wait a minute, wait a minute, hold on, just wait a minute. This is called statistical noise." Goddard said, "Sweetheart, you have a little Black in you." The man replied, "Listen, I'll tell you; oil and water don't mix." Goddard moved to fist bump the man, calling him "Bro." The man refused to fist bump. He later told his local North Dakota newspaper that he doubted the accuracy of the test and said he planned to take more DNA tests and publish the results. "I'll find out with real science and get the whole DNA map," he said. A Black resident of the town close to the White supremacist's enclave told the newspaper, "I knew there was one other Black person in town. Is he going to want to kick out his own self out of town and discriminate against himself?"[13]

Racist Microaggression or Am I Being Too Sensitive?

Most racist acts are microaggressions activated by unconscious biases. I have to guard against labeling any affront to my ego—negative evaluations, being ignored, criticisms, opinions being challenged, denial of requests—as racist. Perhaps there is a better explanation. But it's not always easy, as illustrated in the following experience.

It's a cold day in upstate New York. I am a teaching assistant for a professor at an Ivy League university. Thirty minutes before class, the professor tells me that I would have to give the lecture that day. He had to show important visitors (potential donors to the university) around campus. "Don't panic," I tell myself. (No time to prepare; I had not lectured to this class before.) "What to talk about?" I ask. "Tell them about your master's thesis," he says. I gather my notes, straighten my tie, and walk to the lectern as self-assuredly as I can muster. I look at my students, over 100 of them, all but a handful White (yes, I notice these things), some reading the campus newspaper, many talking to each other, a few glancing up at me. "Where's Professor ... ?" a young man wearing a baseball cap asks loud enough for most to hear. I tell him. Then I hear the strangest sound from many students, a sound I had not heard before. "Hsss . . .."; they were hissing. "What does this mean?" I wonder. Later that day, a friend—born in the United States—explains: "I like to think that the hisses were because the students were disappointed at not having a 'walk' from the lecture, not because a brown-skinned Filipino with an accent, shoulder-length hair, and not much older than them would be teaching them how to be more effective communicators."

So, which explanation is more plausible? Another teaching experience makes me wonder.

Another large class, another time. I am a full-fledged assistant professor, a newly minted PhD, my first semester at a large public university in the Bible Belt, a bastion of conservatism (my friend in Madison had warned me, "Don't go there. I wouldn't go there, and I'm White"). I look no older than my students. I am still brown, my hair is longer, and I am trying to grow a goatee. I have a bruised and swollen lip from a karate sparring competition the day before (which I had won, the local newspaper reported). Three hundred students fill the auditorium. At the conclusion of my lecture on credible communication sources, I remind the students of the final exam. Then came a totally unexpected response from the class: applause. They are applauding me? I thank them. I tell myself, "This is alright!" A group of students approach me at the lecture, thanking me for the semester. One gives me a candy bar. "Thanks for the course," she says, "and congratulations on your trophy."

Racist language, racism in everyday life

Racism has been recorded in the United States since its history began. At an Indian Nations Pow Wow in Coeur d'Alene a few years ago, I spotted an elderly gentleman wearing a T-shirt that read "1492: The first illegal immigrants." I asked him where I could get the T-shirt. The gentleman was White. Until the 1950s signs could be found in California that read "No dogs or Filipinos."[14] In 2019, a poster in Mississippi declared, "This is Klan County. Love it or leave it. Help fight Communism and Integration."[15] At political rallies in 2019, crowds chanted, "Send her back."[16]

In this decade, as recently as 2020, Whites have racially profiled Blacks and other people of color, calling police to investigate innocuous activities in public space. Police question four young Black men waiting for a colleague at a Starbuck's. A White Yale university student calls police when she finds a Black woman napping in the common room of their dorm. Three Black Airbnb guests in Southern California are detained after a White neighbor calls police. A White woman calls police on a Black family barbecuing by a lake in Oakland, California. Applebees apologized and fired three employees for racially profiling three African American customers, falsely accusing them of not paying their checks. At another restaurant, a customer, a White man, tells a waiter to ask a Black family seated close to him to move to another table. A Manhattan attorney scolds restaurant employees for speaking Spanish. He threatens to call immigration officials. A Border Patrol agent detained two women for speaking Spanish at a Montana gas station. In May 2020, a young woman walking her dog in New York City's Central Park calls police and reports that an African American man is threatening her life. The man, a Harvard university alumnus, was bird watching. He had asked the young woman to keep her dog on a leash to comply with park regulations. The police did not issue citations. The young woman is fired from her job. She later apologizes and says she is not a racist. The Harvard graduate says that people should stop threatening the young woman's life and that she may not be a racist but her act was racist.

The list goes on. Social media have captured these racist incidents, many of which have gone viral. For the most part, responses have been supportive of victims. So, what is going on here? Why the profiling? And who are the victims' advocates?

The stories I've told demonstrate the many forms that racism can take, often with tragic results. They also illustrate how complicated racism is and how difficult it is sometimes to label behaviors as racist, with the exception of hate crimes. But make no mistake: Racism exists, in the United States and in every country of the world. I've been a victim; I've been a racist. Perhaps you've been both too, regardless of whether you are White, Black, Brown, or any other color or mixture of colors. You probably have your own stories to tell.

Writing this book made me realize that I have subdued prejudicial feelings and beliefs about people who are not like me or who threaten my identities. Most of these people belong to another race. I am a subconscious racist, never mind that I myself belong to a race that is often, especially now, a target of prejudice in the United States. My racism is subconscious because I am not aware, day to day, that my behaviors and interactions with other people are influenced by race. As an enlightened academic who has marched for civil rights, I am, of course "not a racist." I try very hard not to demonstrate any form of explicit racism in my professional and personal life. But my subconscious racism is another matter. It's more difficult to control. It pops up in the most unlikely of circumstances, such as when I evaluate job candidates for positions at my university or when I evaluate the work of my students. And there's an irony to it all. I stereotype and abhor White racists. But the Implicit Association Test shows I have a slight preference for light over dark skin and that I have a slight subliminal tendency to associate danger and crime with dark skin. The realization that I am a subconscious racist causes stress and discomfort; it is not consistent with my idealized identity or the person I would like to be. It also drives me to control and reduce my subconscious biases, to be mindful of my racism. The good news is that most Americans feel this way. And subconscious racism can be controlled. For most of us, the goal is worth the journey.

This book is about racism—its origins, consequences, and control. Much of the material is based on published scientific research, some of it my own. To illustrate scientific principles, I tell personal stories about my experiences and observations from my viewpoints as a person of color who has experienced racism and as a privileged American who has thought and acted like a racist. I give examples of racism reported in the media and retell stories from friends to bring to life some of the research.

To begin our journey, here are three questions:

- Have you been in a situation where you felt you were treated unfairly because you were "different"?
- Have you treated people unfairly because they were different than you?
- Do you notice the race of people you interact with?

If you answered yes to at least two questions you may be interested in this book. I wrote it for you.

chapter one

Defining Race and Racism

When we talk about racism, we talk about race. And when we talk about race, we talk about racism. Race is a convenient and easy way to distinguish between people who are like us and people who are different. We like people who are similar, dislike people who are different, seek out people who are similar, and avoid people who are different. Some researchers tell us that this instinct is genetically programmed in humans to help us survive in an uncertain environment. Skin color is instantly recognizable and can define difference or similarity in the "blink of an eye."[1] Therefore, most definitions of race are based on skin color and other physical (phenotypic) characteristics that are highly visible. Governments and political elites use race to classify people, often to maintain power, sometimes to ensure that resources are distributed equitably. To the average person, race places people in easily distinguishable categories based on how they look. To racists, these physical characteristics and therefore race define positive and negative personality traits and behaviors. To children, race is an enigmatic concept: They don't know what it is or can't articulate what it is.

When our biracial son was 7, I asked him, "Have people treated you differently because of your race?" He stopped from playing with his Legos blocks, looked at me for a second, returned to building his rocket, and asked, "What do you mean race?"

"Because you look different? Do you notice you are different from most of your classmates and teachers? (He went to a school that was 90% European American.) Your skin color is different."

"Most of my friends and all my teachers have whiter skin. Am I brown or what?"

"It doesn't matter. You are beautifully olive."

"Olive?"

"Does it matter?"

"Some of my friends ask, when Mom picks me up, that's your Mom?!" (A university president interviewing his mom for an administrative position said, upon seeing her, "I did not expect a blonde from Montana." He meant no malice, expecting an Asian given her Asian surname adapted from mine.)

My son's responses are no different from responses of kids his age documented in a number of studies. Children generally do not understand the concept of race and can't or won't define it. However, they do recognize physical differences in people, including skin color, and notice when they or friends are treated differently because they "look different." In one study, White and Hispanic children 7 to 13 years old had difficulty defining race. Black children also had a difficult time but were more likely to define race as differences in skin color. One explanation is that Black parents, in general, talk to their children more often about race to prepare them for prejudice they might face as they grow older. Black and Hispanic children reported more encounters with racial discrimination, which they saw as bad treatment by others because of their skin color. Compared to Black children, Hispanic children reported more discrimination, mostly ethnic slurs.[2] Black and Hispanic children, while having difficulty defining race, had no difficulty recognizing when they were treated poorly and insulted because of their race. Racism was recognized even if the concept of race was fuzzy.

Not only children, but grown-ups running governments have used skin color to define race. Apartheid in South Africa was based on classifying people according to their skin color. People were placed in three categories: "White," "Black," and 'Colored." Whites were descendants of the Dutch ("Afrikaaners") and English colonizers. Blacks were descendants of the native African tribes. Coloreds included people of mixed "races" as well as East Indians and some

Asians. The South African rulers (Afrikaaners and English) used race based on skin color to segregate people, denying economic and political power to Blacks and Coloreds. Marriage between Whites and non-Whites was prohibited; "racial intercourse and any immoral or indecent act" between Whites and non-Whites was a crime; most nonmenial jobs were for Whites only; non-Whites were prohibited from living in White-only neighborhoods. Racism was institutionalized by apartheid based on a superfluous definition of race as skin color. (Trevor Noah gives an insightful commentary of life in apartheid South Africa as a biracial child and young adult.[3])

People in power have used the concept of race throughout human history to oppress people who look different from them, to keep them in their place. They have used skin color, a visible marker of physical differences, to define race because it is a convenient and easy marker. I asked my university students how they defined race, curious whether they shared my view of race as an instrument of oppression.

My students are juniors and seniors from many majors at a large public university. Many have taken history and ethnic studies courses on racism in the United States. In my class, I discuss the consequences of racism on individuals and communities and communication interventions to reduce the harmful effects of bias and prejudice. My class is typically 80% White European American. Many—White and non-White—come from middle- to upper-class families, although more each year are lower-income households first-generation college students. To open the class session on race and racism, I ask my students to identify their race. Most have no difficulty answering "Black," "Hispanic," "Asian," "Pacific Islander," or "White." More each year say "mixed;" some refuse to answer the question. International students mention their region or country of origin.

My next question, "What is race?" is met with hesitancy. The more common answers are as follows:

> "Groups of people that can be distinguished from each other because of physical and cultural characteristics."

> "A person's self-identification as Black, Hispanic, Asian or White."

Less common is this answer, although given with increasing frequency particularly by my Black students:

> "A socially constructed artificial grouping of people
> used by people in power to preserve power."

In a quiz, I would grade all these answers as mostly correct. The
first two definitions echo common usage of race; the third definition
is favored by most scholars doing research on race today.

A student once wrote down a biological definition of race in
a quiz. He defined race as "groups of people who share physical
characteristics because of genetic origin. These characteristics determine how they respond to the environment and are passed on from
generation to generation." He probably got this definition from an
old textbook. I gave him zero points. He asked why I gave him a
"0." I told him that his answer was a biological definition that is
not supported by science. Human beings share about 99.9% of our
genes.[4] Differences in physical characteristics such as skin pigmentation, nasal index, lip form, and the color distribution of body
hair cannot be attributed to genetic differences.[5] Some scientists
attribute these differences to the environment, regional adaptation,
and evolution.[6] Skin color, for example, is determined by climate.
People in the tropics, where human species originated (in sub-Saharan Africa), have darker skin to adapt to greater sunlight intensity.[7]

The biological definition of race has historically been used by
people in power to oppress people they perceived to be different.
This definition says that people who look different because of physical characteristics (phenotype) look different because of genetic
make-up, that phenotypic differences account for differences in
behaviors and abilities, and that these differences—in physical
characteristics, behaviors and abilities—are inherited.

Decades of research by genetic scientists show that the biological
definition has no basis in science. Humans, regardless of phenotype
or geographical origin, share 99.9% of genetic make-up or DNA.
Any two humans, regardless of phenotypic differences (such as a
White man and a Black man) will differ, on average, by 1 in 1,000
in their DNA base. Studies comparing the DNA of populations from
Africa, Asia, Europe, and North and South America, geographical
regions often used in the biological definition to classify people by
race, show that there is 90% DNA variation (of the 1% difference

between humans) in populations in each of these regions, and only 10% separates the populations between regions. Therefore, people belonging to the same "race" show more DNA variation than people classified as being from different races. Some phenotypic differences between people from different races are explained by the environment rather than by genes. Skin color, for example, was primarily determined by climate rather than by genetic make-up.[8]

Eugenics

Race categories have historically been used to enslave, exclude, and exterminate minority groups. Early biological definitions of race, with no scientific evidence, linked physical characteristics to positive and negative behaviors and personality traits. In 1754, a race classification developed by White Europeans considered White Europeans to be "active, acute, [] discoverer[s]" while Black Africans were "crafty, lazy and careless."[9] Use of race as a tool for subjugation and discrimination is illustrated by the eugenics moment, started by Francis Galton in 1883 and still evident in the beliefs of many White supremacists today.[10] Eugenics, sometimes called "scientific racism," is a belief that the "fit" populations of the world are in danger of extinction because of "contamination" from the "unfit" populations. In the United States, according to eugenics, the favored populations are mostly White, born in the United States, and of western European, primarily "Nordic" ancestry. The "unfit" populations included racial groups of color, the poor, the mentally disabled, and immigrants who are "swarthy," "unkempt," and "unassimilable."[11] Eugenics ideology promoted the belief that "unfit" traits were carried by genes and transmitted from generation to generation. Therefore, populations of the "unfits" should be limited to preserve the purity of the "fits." Proponents encouraged benign neglect, forced sterilization, and limited immigration from populations considered unfit. The classification of "fits" and "unfits" generally adhere to racial categories, although they are not explicitly defined as such. At the early inception of eugenics, a "master Nordic race" was the ideal race while races of color were "genetically, ethnically, or socially unfit."[12] Throughout the first 6 decades of the 20th century, hundreds of thousands of Americans were not able to reproduce because of forced sterilization, commitment to mental institutions, and prohibition from marrying.[13] They were selected because of their ancestry, national origin, race, or religion.[14] At the height of its popularity in the early 1900s , eugenics was supported in the United States by prominent academics, philanthropists, and politicians, including representatives from the Carnegie Institution; the Rockefeller Foundation; Harvard, Princeton, and Yale universities; the American Medical Association; Margaret Sanger; Oliver Wendel Holmes; and Woodrow Wilson.[15] Historically, eugenics was evident in the Nazi extermination of Jews (Hitler was an admirer of eugenics), apartheid South Africa, and the subjugation of native peoples by European and American colonizers.

Eugenics is not overtly or explicitly promoted as a racial ideology in the United States today. However, many of its ideas can be found in White supremacist ideologies that promote the preservation of "White culture" upheld as "superior" to non-White cultures.[16] Whether some public policies, such as immigration, intentionally or coincidentally, promote eugenics ideology is open for discussion.

A biological definition of race is central to the construction of eugenics as racist ideology. Most scientists today believe that biological race is an artificial, ephemeral classification of humans created by people holding economic and political power who wish to maintain that power. Therefore, race is "socially constructed" with no biological basis, defined at any given point in history by people in power. Examples can be found in U.S. history. In 1830, the U.S. Census included the following categories: free White persons (not a slave, no detectable or visible sub-Saharan or American Indian ancestry, of West European ancestry) and free colored person (with detectable sub-Saharan ancestry, not free.) In 1890, the U.S. Census categories changed as people migrated to the United States. The 1890 categories were White (European ancestry), Black (sub-Saharan), Quadroon (1/4 sub-Saharan), Octoroon (1/8 sub-Saharan), Chinese, Japanese, American Indian.[17] These categories were based on self-reports, documentation of ancestry, and how a person looked. They were used by people in power (mostly Whites) to determine activities and rights, such as voting, of other groups.

Current Definitions of Race

Decades of research have shown that physical attributes of race and related characteristics, such as intelligence, cannot be explained by genetic differences.[18] Most current definitions do not consider race to be a biological construct based on genetic make-up. The U.S. Census Bureau, for example, currently defines race as a person's self-identification with one or more social groups, which are then listed. This definition refers to social groups based on ancestry or current geographical origins. On a census questionnaire, we are first asked whether we are Hispanic. Hispanic is defined as "Mexican, Mexican American, Chicano, Puerto Rican, Cuban or another Hispanic, Latino or other Spanish origin." The next question asks us to identify as one of the following: White alone; Black or African American alone; American Indian or Alaska Native alone; Asian alone—Asian Indian, Japanese, Chinese, Korean, Vietnamese, Filipino, other Asian; Native Hawaiian or Other Pacific Islander; Guamanian or Chamorro; Some Other Race; Two or More Races."

The U.S. Census accounts for groups residing in the United States, referring to the groups as "race." These categories, based on geographic origin, include the following:

> White: Europe, the Middle East, North Africa
>
> Black or African American: Africa
>
> American Indian or Alaska native: North America, South America, Central America
>
> Asian: Far East, Southeast Asia, Indian
>
> Native Hawaiian or other Pacific Islander: Hawaii, Guam, Samoa, Pacific Islands

The U.S. Census Bureau defines race as socially constructed and based on self-identification. In theory, these categories, although called "race," do not subscribe to the assumption of biological race that traits and behavioral predispositions are inherited. The U.S. Census categories count the many groups in the United States according to geographical origin, including immigrants. There are many categories because the United States is a country of immigrants from many different regions of the world. In 2017, immigrants who were U.S. citizens or permanent residents accounted for almost 14% of the U.S. population. Most immigrants came from South and East Asia (27%), followed by Mexico (25%), Europe/Canada (13%), the Caribbean (10%), Central America (8%), South America (7%), the Middle East (4%) and sub-Saharan Africa (4%). Mexico was the top origin country, followed by China, India, the Philippines, and El Salvador.[19] The U.S. Census accounts for the new immigrant groups as well as "older" established groups such as "White" Europeans.

The U.S. Census uses many "racial" categories because policy makers such as elected officials use the data to make funding decisions that affect educational opportunities, assess equal employment practices, and ensure equal access to health care.[20] The U.S. Census Bureau does not share respondent answers with immigration law enforcement, tax collection agencies, or any other organization.

Based on self-identification and geographical origin, the U.S. Census categories illustrate how the meanings of "race" change with time either as an instrument of benevolence or, more often, exploitation. To simplify racial categories, public discourse often uses skin color to identify people. In the United States, "White" and "people of color" are often used when we talk about racism. People of color are Browns and Blacks. In this simplified scheme, the diversity in cultures within each color category is lost. A common assumption is that people who are White are one race; people who are not White, although from different geographical regions, are another "race." Even though science tells us that these are artificial categories created for specific purposes, they are in common usage because they are convenient, saving us the time and effort required to know and evaluate people as individuals. Scientists use racial categories to develop interventions to mitigate the harmful effects of racism. Governments, businesses, and social institutions use race to conveniently subdivide large populations into manageable subgroups to preserve power, authority, dominance, and control,[21] and in some cases to distribute resources equitably. Individuals use race to simplify a complex environment, to guide social interactions, and to decide whom to approach and to avoid. Regardless of its utility, race is a scientifically invalid construct.

Racism

Race does not exist, but racism does.

In its simplest and most destructive form, racism is the belief that people can be grouped according to physical attributes such as skin pigmentation, nasal index, lip form, color distribution, and texture of body hair;[22] that each group exhibits positive and negative traits and behavioral predispositions; that physical attributes and genes determining traits and behaviors are passed on to each generation; and that societies must control races with "negative" traits to protect races with "positive" traits. This definition of racism was used by proponents of the biological definition and eugenics.[23]

Most Americans today will not admit to being a racist, especially a biological racist. Many societies and governments, certainly the United States, profess to be egalitarian and to value equality. Therefore, it is not socially desirable to admit to being a racist. Social scientists have developed definitions of racism that do not require admission of support for the biological definition, but instead ask for support of opinions and actions resulting from acceptance of racial categories. Most modern definitions ask about consequences of racial categories, that is, perceptions of other people and resulting behaviors, rather than the biological origins. These definitions say that racism assumes certain racial groups, as commonly used in a society, are inferior to other groups and that this difference justifies unequal treatment. Individuals can be racist, but so can institutions and cultures. For individuals, racism is defined today as opinions and behavioral intentions that differentiate between individuals because of a category presumed to be "race." This differentiation places certain individuals, because of their perceived group category, in disadvantaged positions such as having less access to resources, experiencing unequal treatment, and having greater chances of being victims of violence as in hate crimes. When individual beliefs about "racial" differences are translated into laws and government policies, then we have institutional racism, as in apartheid and Jim Crow laws. Racist beliefs that are reinforced in popular media and everyday life (microaggressions) and are embedded in the collective thinking and actions of a community, overt or subconsciously, result in cultural racism. Racism is systemic when it is demonstrated by individuals, institutionalized, and culturally reinforced. No citizen or government official will admit to being racist in America today.

The evidence, of course, tells otherwise. Instead of asking, we look for symptoms or markers. Hate crimes, including the killings of unarmed Black men and women, are a visible marker. More difficult to detect are demonstrations of nonviolent racism, often negative opinions and stereotypes of victims that direct behaviors toward and evaluations of them.

More than 40 years ago, social psychologist Gordon Allport proposed four stages of racism.[24] The first stage is "antilocution," or talk about a target group that expresses unwarranted (no supporting evidence) negative evaluations about a racial group. This talk often happens in small group conversations among people who agree on the negative evaluations, frequently in social media. Virulent and incendiary language is used, as in chat rooms and internet sites of hate groups. But "average" people also engage in this conversation. Examples are referring to Blacks as thugs or drug dealers or calling them lazy; Hispanic immigrants as illegals or rapists; Asian Americans as predators; and Native Americans as drunks. Language sets the stage for deadly consequences of racism. The extermination of Jews in Nazi Germany was stoked by people who denigrated Jews.

The next stage of racism is avoidance. Certain groups may be barred from a country because of biases based on race. The third stage is discrimination. Groups are denied rights and access to resources such as voting, health care, education. The fourth stage is physical attack. Examples are killings of innocent men because they are Black. And the last stage is extermination, such as the Holocaust, "ethnic cleansing" in Rwanda, and wars against Indigenous populations.

Racism Toward Blacks in America

Although it's not socially acceptable to overtly say that Blacks are inferior to Whites, racism is demonstrated when innocent and unarmed Black men and women are 2.5 times more likely than innocent and unarmed Whites to be shot dead by police officers. More generally, individual and institutional perceptions result in actions that discriminate against Blacks by withholding community resources or by subjecting Blacks to different standards of behaviors compared to Whites.

National polls consistently show that majorities of Whites in the United States express negative attitudes toward Blacks. In 2012, 4 years after we elected out first Black president, 51% of all Americans expressed anti-Black attitudes compared to 48% four years ago. Anti-Black attitudes were measured by the Modern Racism Scale. People who endorse modern racism believe that racism against Blacks is a thing of the past; Blacks are too pushy in demanding their rights; this pushiness results in unfair tactics; and the advances Blacks have made are undeserved.[25] Another national poll showed that 36% of Blacks said they had been discriminated against in the past year, compared to 20% of Hispanics and 10% of Whites.[26]

Negative attitudes toward Blacks lead to life threatening consequences. National statistics show that five times as many Whites use drugs as Blacks. Yet Blacks comprise the great majority of drug offenders sent to prison. Black men are 13 times more likely to be sent to prison on drug charges than are White men.[27] In another study, 70% of the drivers stopped by state troopers in Maryland in 1 year were Black, yet only 17.5% of all cited speeders were Black.[28] Still another study shows that Blacks are more likely than Whites to receive the death penalty, particularly when the defendant has stereotypically Black features and when the victim is White.[29]

Racism is demonstrated every day. A group of Blacks were asked to change tables at a Chicago restaurant because a regular customer did "not want to sit around Black people."[30] A young Black man was taken to a New York city police precinct after paying for a belt at a fashion store because the sales clerk doubted he could afford the belt.[31] No persons involved in these situations admitted to being a racist. However, their actions demonstrate racism. Blacks were victimized by police officers, judges, juries, sales clerks, and "average" people—almost all of whom were White—because of the color of their skin.

Stereotypes

Racism is influenced by preconceptions about victimized groups, preconceptions that people in a group share similar traits and behavioral tendencies. Some groups are assigned positive traits and behaviors; others are assigned negative traits and behaviors, which are a basis for racism. These generalized traits are stereotypes.

We use labels to organize what can be a chaotic world. We label objects, people, and tasks on our to-do lists. A label helps us decide what to do with a thing once we have attached a label to it. We assume that things in a label share certain characteristics that save us from evaluating each thing that is in the label. We respond to the label, not the individual item. I've used labels to organize tasks I have to do in my everyday and professional life. The labels I use are "Priority 1" (do now), "Priority 2" (do tomorrow), and "Priority 3" (can wait).

Stereotypes are labels we attach to people. The label can be based on profession (physician, professor, police officer), physical attractiveness, age, gender, or any other group membership that will guide our evaluations of and behaviors toward individuals we encounter every day. We encounter an individual, place them in a group, and respond according to our preconceptions (or "mental picture") of the group. Group members share group characteristics. This saves us the trouble of getting to know people as individuals.[32]

Stereotypes and Racism

Most stereotypes of non-White groups ("races") in the United States are negative. When negative traits and behavioral tendencies are generalized to all members of a race, and when this generalization affects the treatment of racial members in a community, then racism is the result.

Stereotypes of Minority Races

A national poll representative of the U.S. adult population asked respondents, "How well does each of these words (stereotypic trait) describe most (racial group)—extremely well, very well, moderately well, slightly well, not at all, or refuse to answer?" The results show that most people actually were not willing to explicitly assign negative traits to racial groups; most responses were "not at all" for negative traits or "slightly well" for positive traits. However, some racial groups were rated less positively or more negatively on some of the traits. For example, Whites were perceived to be more likely than Blacks and Hispanics to be friendly, determined to succeed, law-abiding, intelligent at school, smarter at everyday things, good neighbors, and dependable; likely to keep up property; to be complaining; and to be boastful. Blacks were stereotyped to be more likely than Whites to be less friendly, less determined to succeed, less hardworking, less intelligent at school, less smart at everyday things, less likely to be good neighbors, less likely to keep up property, and less dependable and more likely to be violent, lazy, and irresponsible. Hispanics compared to Whites were less friendly, less law-abiding, less intelligent at school, less smart at everyday things, and less likely to keep up property. Hispanics were also more hard working, less lazy, less complaining, and less boastful.[33]

Most people in the poll rated all racial groups positively. However, Whites were rated more positively than the other groups on almost all of the traits.

Another poll of 39,000 Americans showed that Asian Americans and Whites were rated to be the most peaceful; Muslims and Muslim Americans were rated to be the most violent with little difference between the two groups, followed by Blacks. Asian Americans and Whites were rated to be most trustworthy; Muslim and Muslim Americans were rated to be the most untrustworthy (with little difference); Blacks were the only group to be rated as lazy, although their negative ratings were close to the midpoint (neutral). All other groups were rated to be hard-working, with Asian Americans receiving the highest ratings.[34]

Results of recent studies are consistent. Americans assign positive traits to all racial groups. However, Whites are rated more positively on most traits. These differences may reveal how other groups are perceived. Since it's not socially desirable to rate Blacks as "violent," I can still say that Whites are less violent. It's difficult to measure how we actually feel about other groups when we are asked directly about our feelings and perceptions. We are conscious of what, in an egalitarian society, the "correct" answers should be.

Unconscious Racism

Most Americans are not overt or conscious racists. They do not admit that they commit racist acts because they are racist. However, most Americans—up to 80%—have unconscious racial biases that lead them to commit everyday racist acts.[35] They are unconscious biases because we may not even be aware that we have them. These biases include the association of certain traits or stereotypes to races. Unconscious biases or feelings and stereotypes are stored in long-term memory. They develop through time from accumulated bits of information from socialization agents such as the media, peers, parents, teachers, and the community. Most of the time, information about racial differences is incomplete, inaccurate, or self-serving. Nevertheless, this information leads to impressions of other groups, which we do not acknowledge explicitly. Unconscious biases and stereotypes are automatically activated (we don't ordinarily control their activation) when "triggered" by cues or primes in our environment. The presence of a member of a racial group is an example of a cue or prime. An automatic activation may take the form of an instant overall assessment of the individual based on their race or behavior toward the individual. My unconscious stereotype of Blacks, for example, might be that they are aggressive and violent. This stereotype may be triggered by the sight of a Black man late at night walking on a sidewalk toward me. My unconscious stereotype then leads me to cross the street to avoid him.

Uncovering Unconscious Biases

One way of uncovering unconscious biases is through introspection. In 30 seconds, what adjectives come to mind when you think of a Black man? A Hispanic man? A Middle Eastern woman? A White man? This isn't easy to do because we are aware of the "proper" answers. A more accurate way is to take an Implicit Association Test (IAT). The IAT was developed in the mid-1990s by psychologists to measure our implicit biases against groups of people—race, gender, age, sexual orientation, national origin, and dozens of other groups. The test requires the test taker to click on a computer keyboard response that correspond to a "stimulus" (member of a racial group, for example). Responses could be positive or negative words or images. Responses are measured in milliseconds. The less time it takes to make an association (clicking on a word or image), the stronger the association. For example, consider a photo of a young Black American man as the stimulus and photos of a gun and reading glasses as a response. If it takes me less time to associate the gun with the photo, then my unconscious stereotype of Black men with violence would be activated. This is an oversimplification of the IAT. You might want to take the test yourself by logging on to

Implicit Harvard. It's free. You will receive your results and won't be identified, but you will have to agree that your results will be aggregated with others who take the test for research purposes. Some IAT results have shown over 60% of test takers favored European Americans; about 10% favored African Americans, and 24% were neutral. Most test takers had more positive evaluations of lighter skin over darker skin, and most associated Black faces with weapons and White faces with harmless objects.[36] Most people who take the IAT are not overt racists. They want to find out more about their feelings toward other people and are generally open-minded with more education than the general population. It's revealing, therefore, that large majorities still reveal implicit biases.

Limitations of the IAT

Some critics say that the cut-off points on who is neutral, slightly biased, moderately biased, and strongly biased are arbitrary and have low correlations to actual discriminatory behaviors. But defenders say that the IAT is still the best measure of racism and stereotyping and that results actually predict certain behaviors. We cannot identify racists by asking them; they won't admit to it. We can, however, define racist behaviors and use results from the IAT to make connections between these behaviors and unconscious biases and stereotypes.

My Subconscious Stereotyping of Racists

I've learned not to stereotype racists.

After a workout in our dojo (training hall), our sensei (martial arts teacher) takes me aside and asks if I would like to teach a class at a community center in a neighboring, rural town. We are in West Texas, a bastion of conservative social, political, and religious thought, where gun racks in pick-up trucks are a common sight and a "macho" male-centric culture is the norm—and was the perfect place for racists, I had thought at that time. My studying the martial arts was very much a response to my new environment.

"Yes, of course," I say without hesitation (you don't say no to your sensei). "I like teaching kids."

"Your students won't be kids."

"That's fine. Adults are good too."

"Your students will be members of the Wild Boars."

I pause. That's a motorcycle gang. I had images of the Hell's Angels, burly men with White power and Nazi tattoos, bald heads and unkempt beards, drug dealers or worse, racists too who would not hesitate to beat me up. "Why would I teach them the martial arts? They already have guns and knives. We should be teaching their victims, Black and Brown people." I was trying to find a way out. I was thinking, "Why me? A Brown Filipino with a ponytail. Ask one of the White black belts to teach those rednecks."

A week later, I park in front of the community center. It was not a community center. It was the gang's clubhouse. Twenty or so men, mostly in their 30s and 40s, all shapes and sizes, all White, were waiting for me, some sitting on the floor, others standing or leaning on the walls, most engaged in animated conversation. I am wearing my black gi and my well-worn brown belt. "I know more of this stuff than any of you will ever know," I thought, trying to build my confidence. No one notices me when I enter the room.

"Hello!" I say loudly without shouting. Wouldn't "Hey" or "Yo" be more appropriate?

Most of the conversation stops. The men turn toward me.

I introduce myself ("I'm Bruce Lee, reincarnated; don't mess with me" was what I wanted to say—thank goodness for Asian stereotypes). I tell them I'm glad to be their teacher. I ask them to form two lines facing me, to take off their shoes and boots (we're in Texas), and to introduce themselves and say why they are interested in the martial arts and what they did for a living. I get the usual answers to my first question—to stay in shape, for self-defense. Some say for harmony, inner peace. Answers to my second question provide the surprise. They are accountants, store owners, farmers, ranchers, school teachers, a lawyer or two. No Hells Angels.

I enjoy teaching the class and go out for a beer with some of my students after our workout.

Preference for Whiteness

Inherent in any discussion of racism is the notion of racial hierarchy. An interesting phenomenon is the "preference for Whiteness" in the United States and some other countries. Skin color is used by people in these countries to assign worth or value, consciously or subconsciously, particularly by people from races in power (mostly White) but also less frequently by people who are victims of prejudice. The result is racism, with lighter-skinned groups (such as White European Americans) at the top of the hierarchy and darker-skinned groups (such as Black Americans) at the bottom: the lighter the skin, the higher regard for the person and their group, resulting in differential privilege, opportunities, and benefits. When the preference for Whiteness is pervasive in a culture (such as in popular media), the favored people and their groups are reinforced for explicit or subconscious beliefs that "White is better." Except for fringe White supremacists and neo-Nazis, White racial superiority is not endorsed openly in America today. However, historical examples of White superiority racism can be found from around the world as well as the United States: eugenics, apartheid South Africa, slavery, the subjugation of Native Americans, slavery, Jim Crow.

Apartheid in South Africa is worth revisiting since it remains a sick example of institutional racism based on White supremacy: The purpose of apartheid was to preserve the power of White rulers, keep the non-White "natives" in their places of subjugation, and foment divisions among the ruled to prevent them from gaining power in numbers.[37] Apartheid, in place from 1948 to 1984, "the state of being apart," classified groups ("races") into three categories based on skin color: Whites were descendants of Dutch (Afrikaners) and English colonizers; Blacks were descendants of the Indigenous African tribes; coloreds included people of mixed races (often with White fathers and Black mothers), East Indians, and some Asians. Race or color laws were enacted to subjugate and separate non-Whites. Most nonmenial jobs were for Whites only. Blacks and coloreds were prohibited from living in White-only neighborhoods. Rights and privileges depended on skin color. At the top were Whites. Coloreds, who generally had lighter skin tone than Indigenous Africans, had more privileges than Blacks. They did not have to carry documents required of Blacks.

To preserve the "purity" of the White races, marriage or any other intimate relations between Whites and non-Whites was prohibited. Infractions often resulted in jailtime for the Black or colored person, particularly if he was male, and reprimand for the White person, particularly if he was male.[38] (I was an honorary White in apartheid South Africa for a week, there to lecture, so I could stay with my wife in the same hotel room.)

With the enactment of the Civil Rights Act of 1964, prohibiting discrimination based on race, color, religion, sex or national origin, explicit racism is illegal in the United States. However, White preference (sometimes called White privilege) is evident: racial profiling, the unequal distribution of resources, health care disparities, inequities in the administration of justice and law enforcement, and the killings of innocent Black men. In the past few decades, social scientists have studied subconscious racism as expressions of White privilege. For example, Whites and, less frequently, some people of color attribute higher status, power, and wealth to Whites; light skin is generally considered by White people to be more attractive than dark skin.

The preference for Whiteness by Whites can be interpreted simply as expressions of identity and pride in who they are. However, this preference, explicit or implicit, when used to elevate Whiteness over color can lead to negative evaluations of and behaviors toward non-Whites. Results from Implicit Association Tests show that darker skin is more likely than lighter skin to be associated with crime and danger. Job candidates perceived to be White from their names are more likely to be called for interviews compared to job candidates perceived to be Black from their names. Black video game characters are more likely to be shot and in less time than White characters in equivalent scenarios. Blacks are more likely than Whites to receive the death penalty. Within a race, skin tone affects life outcomes. Darker-skinned Blacks, compared to lighter-skinned Blacks, have lower levels of education, income and job status,[39] plausibly because they face less discrimination from the dominant White group. Immigrants to the United States with the lightest skin earned an average of 8% to 15% more than did immigrants with darker skin after accounting for country of origin, proficiency in English, occupation, and education—again, plausibly because they face less discrimination.[40] The greatest wage differential (10% to 15%) between American Blacks and Whites in the same jobs was between Whites with dark or medium-dark skin.[41] Blacks with darker skin and stereotypically Black features were more likely to receive the death penalty when the victim was White, compared to less stereotypical Blacks who who were less likely to receive the death penalty.[42]

Recognizing that skin tone makes a difference in American society, the 1995 Federal Glass Ceiling Commission concluded,

> Color-based differences are inescapable in American society but nobody likes to talk about them. Though it is mostly covert, our society has developed an extremely sophisticated, and often denied, acceptability index based on gradations in skin color. It is applied to African Americans, American Indians, Asian and Pacific Islanders, to Hispanic Americans.[43]

Color-based racism, though generally not overtly practiced, is all too common in the United States today. It can also be found in other countries expressed as a preference for Whiteness.

In some East Asian countries, many young people consider White skin more attractive (beautiful) than dark skin. For example, about two thirds of men in a Hong Kong survey said they preferred women who had fair skin. Almost half of young adults said they used skin whiteners. Many Asians consider White skin to be indicative of racial or group superiority in their populations.[44]

Many young adults in South Asia equate White skin with beauty and high social status and dark skin with low social and economic status. Advertisements for some skin bleaching products, for example, suggest that darker-skinned women have "a problem" in seeking jobs or marriage, and the solution is to lighten their skin tone with the advertised product.[45]

In some Latin American countries, light skin is considered by many to be more attractive than dark skin. People with light skin are generally portrayed in the media and advertisements as powerful, socially privileged, and desirable while people with dark skin are in subservient roles. Many popular film and television actors and actresses have light skin and European facial features.

Why the Preference for Whiteness?

The notion that Whiteness is preferable and that White races are superior has its roots in Europe. In 1785, an anatomist and naturalist from Germany proposed a racial hierarchy on the basis of "perceived superiority beauty" and closeness to the "ideal." At the top of the hierarchy were White Europeans; at the bottom were Africans and Asians. Presumed White superiority found advocates among politicians and religious leaders who interpreted Judeo-Christian scripture as suggesting that Europeans were "the chosen people" of God, a basis for the principle of "manifest destiny," which said that it was the duty of Europeans to reclaim the world "in God's name." Of course, manifest destiny was conveniently used by European colonizers seeking riches and land while subjugating and annihilating darker-skinned native populations in the "new world."[46]

In the United States, some scholars attribute the preference for Whiteness to the fact that White Americans hold most positions of power in business, government, education, the media, and other institutions. To preserve this power, White Americans consciously or unconsciously adapt the "White is good" ideal. White supremacist groups proclaim this ideal overtly. Most Americans deny this ideology as racist but subconsciously accept it. Subconscious acceptance is cumulatively reinforced by the media—television, film, magazines, newspapers, advertisements—which influence our ideas about what is beautiful and good. Although there has been significant improvement in the diversity of images in the past 10 years, the beauty and goodness standard continues to be "Whiteness."

For many people in former European and American colonies, the association of Whiteness with power, beauty, and wealth is a product of the colonial experience. White Europeans and Americans introduced (some historians say forced) their cultures, religions, and governments to Indigenous populations. The colonizers had military and economic power and represented themselves as ideal and "civilized" societies, a better alternative to the native cultures they found, while enriching themselves. Through time, the colonial ideal seeped into the consciousness of many colonized peoples, with some noteworthy exceptions of rebellion. For many, however, the ideal was the "mother country," which was White. Even today, in many former European and American colonies, much of the wealth and power, handed down from generation to generation, is found among descendants of the colonizers. These descendants, even some who have intermarried with Indigenous populations, have lighter skin.

Another explanation for the preference for Whiteness in some countries is the ubiquity of American media—television and films particularly—around the world. Access is facilitated by the internet and satellites, particularly among young people. The images projected, with few exceptions, are of a White, wealthy, hedonistic and free society, desirable to many people abroad, particularly young people. When Americans of color are portrayed, they are often criminals and drug dealers and are poor.[47]

To most of the world, American is White. I am rarely an "American" when I travel abroad. There are some countries where American and Whiteness are not preferred. Is it politics or racism?

I am standing in line for security check at the Cairo airport after spending 2 days exploring the pyramids and other antiquity sites on my way to Jordan to give a lecture. I notice that most passengers go through routine screening, body scanners, and some patting, while others are selected for more intensive checks, including an interrogation. The security officer at my gate, a middle-aged woman wearing a hijab, smiles as I hand her my passport and boarding pass. "Filipino?" she asks. "No," I say too quickly. "American." Her smile disappears and she points me toward the line for intensive screening. I wondered while I waited in line, "Why did I say American?" In the United States, I am often asked, "But where do you really come from?"

chapter two

Why Does Racism Exist?

Daryl Davis is a Black musician who attended Ku Klux Klan rallies because of an incident in his childhood. When he was 10 years old he participated in a parade as a cub scout in his mostly White hometown. He carried the American flag. As the scouts walked through town, young Daryl was pelted by rocks, pop cans, and bottles, causing injuries to his face. He thought he was being hit because some people did not like Cub Scouts. But he was the only scout being hit. His mother and father later explained to him that he was a target because of the color of his skin. Young Daryl asked his parents, "How can they hate me when they don't even know me?" Because of this experience, Daryl Dawkins vowed that he would try to understand racial hatred. And that is why, as an adult, he attended Klan rallies with a KKK grand dragon who later would become his friend and who would walk away from the Klan. Mr. Davis tells his remarkable story in a TEDx Napperville talk in 2017 (ted.com/talks/daryl_davis_why_i_as_a_black_man_attend_kkk_rallies).

Why does racism exist? Scientists have been trying to answer this question for decades. Several explanations have been proposed. Racism is used by groups in power to maintain power. Racism is hard-wired into humans as an instrument of survival. Racism is a product of the environment. These explanations do not condone racism. They are attempts at understanding racism so that solutions can be found and implemented.

A Biological Explanation Discredited

One explanation is that humans and other animal species are hard-wired or programmed to be racist. To survive, a species has to protect its gene pool to keep the species "pure." One way is to keep other species away. Racism is a defense; other races are a threat. Through evolution, an aversion to other species is hard-wired into the genetic make-up of humans. This biological explanation of racism has two problems. First is the equivalence made between "other species" and "race." As we have seen, race is an artificial concept that has no biological correspondence. And second, a biological definition is deterministic: We are born racists and there's nothing we can do about it.[1] A strictly biological explanation of racism is no longer accepted by scientists.

Racism Is a Product of the Environment

Most scientists today analyze the influence of the environment on the development of racial biases. For example, they study at what age babies recognize race and develop preferences for the same race. They look at the babies' environment for clues that might explain race preferences. These clues include the race of caregivers. A consistent finding is that newborn babies do not express a racial preference, but by the time they are 3 months old they express a visual preference for same race faces.[2] As one noted psychologist asked, "Why do some babies grow up to be racists while other babies grow up to be activists for racial justice?"

How Racial Preferences Are
Detected Among Babies

Researchers use a visual-preference (VP) task procedure for studying newborn infants and babies up to 6 months. Researchers project photos of faces representing different racial groups on a screen. A camera records eye movements of the baby, which are counted by a computer. Looking times indicate a preference for a face. In studies in the United States and the United Kingdom, Caucasian (White) babies consistently spend more time looking at Caucasian faces compared to faces of people from other ethnic groups by 3 months old. There are no differences from birth until 3 months. In a United Kingdom study, the researchers used photos of adult men who were Caucasian, Middle Eastern, African, and Asian.[3]

According to the researchers, babies will show a visual preference for faces to whom they have been exposed. A consistent finding is that babies who are cared for by a woman show a visual preference for women, while babies cared for by a man show a visual preference for men.[4] The same explanation can be used for racial visual preferences. In almost all of the research, Caucasians (White) babies who had little or no exposure to faces who were not White were studied. According to these studies, babies at birth have no preference for faces based on race but learn these preferences within the first 3 months of life. They learn to prefer faces with whom they are predominantly exposed to. And typically these are faces from their own race. Studies have shown, for example, that over 90% of people that infants interact with are of their own race.[5] The conclusion is that visual racial preferences are learned at a very early age through exposure to people.

Racial Preferences as Babies
Get Older

There is evidence that babies, as they get older, show other racial preferences besides a visual preference. For example, 6- to 9-month-old babies associate faces from their own races with happy music and faces from other races with sad music. And they learn more from adults from their own race than adults from other races.[6] These findings, like the visual preference for their own race in younger babies, are explained by early exposure to people. People—adults and other babies—that babies are exposed to in early life, particularly if other people are nurturing, will influence facial preferences, associations with positive feelings, and learning. Babies pick up on these cues and are able to recognize facial features at a very early age, as young as 3 months. Skin color is a feature that they recognize.[7]

As children get older, their environment continues to influence their perceptions of people from their own and different races. "Race" is identified by skin color and facial characteristics. Children soak in their environment. They observe who does what—teachers, doctors, neighbors, sales clerks, cleaners, and police officers. Because the physical characteristics often associated with race, such as skin color, are easily observed, children will form expectations of what people do from what they see every day and the skin color of the people they observe.

The everyday experiences of children growing up suggest that certain roles and relationships are based on race. For example, White children growing up in mostly White neighborhoods may notice that people have different heights, ages, and genders but mostly the same skin color. They may then, following the baby studies, develop a preference for "White" over other skin colors because White is "normal," "right," and comfortable. When children learn by observation they form conclusions about race and skin color based on these observations.[8] They don't have to be directly told that certain races are preferable to other races and that there is a "place" for people based on their race. They can form these conclusions by observation.

Parents and Caregivers Influence

Racial Preferences of Children

A logical expectation is that racist parents or caregivers will raise racist children. Early research has been contradictory. Some studies showed strong parental influence while others did not. More recently, results have been clearer. Parents who are racially biased, implicitly or explicitly, generally will raise children who will also be racially biased when children strongly identify with them. This influence can be communicated directly, as in "Don't play with him or her," or indirectly, such as when the behaviors and parents' language are observed and adapted by the child. On the other hand, parents who talk to children about why racism is "not good" and whose behaviors and language support this assertion will generally raise children who are less racist when children strongly identify with them. What is important is how strongly children identify with their parents. Not surprisingly, stronger identification leads to more influence.[9]

To measure identification with parents, researchers ask questions such as "How much do you care about making your parents proud?" "How often do you do what your parents tell you to do?" "How much do you enjoy spending time with a parent?" and "How much would you like to be like your parent?"[10]

The Media Influence Children's Perceptions of Race

As children grow older, they encounter people from other races and learn how to think of them from the media. With laptops, tablets, iPhones, and other digital devices available to children at an early age, a whole new world opens up beyond what they can directly experience or observe. This world is delivered by the media. The internet has made delivery easy and convenient. Television, movies, newspapers, magazines, and books are sources of information about other races. Children learn from the media what is "right" and "normal," the norms of their communities. These norms include perceptions of other races. Despite the efforts of many media organizations and recent improvements, the portrayals of racial minorities in U.S. media, particularly movies and television, are still predominantly and stereotypically negative.

Media Portray Minorities Negatively

Recent studies have shown that just about every racial minority in the United States is portrayed negatively in the media.[11]

Asian Americans are depicted in stereotypical occupations such as restaurant workers, Korean grocers, Japanese businessmen, Indian cab drivers, TV anchorwomen, martial artists, gangsters, faith healers, laundry workers, and prostitutes. Asian racial features, names, accents, and mannerisms are parodied as comic and sinister; Asians are cast in supporting roles in movies and television with primarily Asian or Asian American content; Asian male sexuality is predatory or nonexistent; Asian women are exotic, subservient, compliant, and eager to please; Asians are foreigners, not American.[12]

Hispanics are often portrayed in news and entertainment as criminals or gang members, gardeners or landscapers, maids or housekeepers, or high school dropouts.[13]

African Americans in news and entertainment are violent, engaged in criminal activity, use vulgar profanity, and are immoral, athletic, and to be feared.[14]

Native Americans are wise elders and are often aggressive, drunk, obese, impoverished drug addicts.

Arab Americans, Arabs, and Muslims are often portrayed as evil, terrorists and attackers who cause explosions or are pursuing fun, lust, and extravagance, a threat to the United States.[15]

Media Stereotypes Are Not Accurate Portrayals

Some members of stereotyped racial groups might fit the stereotype. The problem is when these stereotypes are presented as representative of the entire group and we can certainly make the case that this is not true. For example, most drug users in the United States are White, not Black, as proportions of their populations.[16] When there is no other information available either from personal contact or media portrayals, these negative stereotypes are used to define races, influencing our actions toward members of the race. Children, in particular, are vulnerable to forming group impressions based on what they see and hear in the media, though adults are also influenced.

Media Stereotypes Influence Our Stereotypes of Racial Groups

There is consistent evidence that negative stereotypes, and in comparison to positive stereotypes, are remembered more easily and are more influential. Negative portrayals arouse emotions in less time. So people are more likely to pay attention and are more likely to be influenced. In one study of 3,000 non-Latino Americans, people who saw negative television clips of Hispanics, such as gang activity, were more likely to say that, in the real world, Hispanics were gang members, use welfare, take jobs away from Americans, and were illegal immigrants compared to people who did not see the negative TV clips.[17]

Media Stereotypes of Minorities Are Mostly Negative

There has been some improvement in the portrayals of racial minorities in the past decade. However, negative stereotypes remain because writers and producers write and create "what they know," and most writers, creative people, producers, and editors are White, especially in mainstream media.[18] This is not to say that only members of a racial group could know about that group. Nonmembers can learn about a group with time, effort, and the proper motivation. An approach that has worked, in addition to having more diversity among the ranks of writers, producers, and editors, is to enlist the expertise of consultants from the racial group.

Another reason for negative stereotypes in the media is structural constraints. Media people work under time, space, and resource constraints that often result in doing things as they've always done before, using routines and practices that often result in biased coverage and biased portrayals of groups they are not familiar with. There are exceptions, such as well-researched documentaries and long-form stories (historically, Edward R. Murrow's *Harvest of Shame* comes to mind).

Yet another reason for negative stereotyping is that in a democracy with a free and generally unsubsidized press, media are a business. Media have to make a profit to survive. To be profitable, news and entertainment media need to attract the largest possible audiences in their demographic markets so that they, in turn, can attract advertisers. Considerable audience research analyzes what audiences want and how to balance audience preferences with the public good. From a social identity perspective, we can interpret audience preferences in the context of out-groups and in-groups, and the human need for reinforcement of self and group identities. One way of doing this is to hold one's group—such as race—to be superior to others. We need villains and heroes and heroines. And out-groups such as minority races are convenient villains. Villains in American entertainment have included, at one time or another, African Americans, Native Americans, the Japanese, Russians, Chinese, Arabs, Latinos and other racial groups.[19]

Contributing to the "media as a business" explanation is the changing audience for news and entertainment. The way people process media information has dramatically changed in the past decade with common use of digital media and mobile devices. Young people, in particular, have shorter attention spans than older adults. People in general consume news and entertainment on the move, often multitasking and seldom focusing on any particular media activity at any given time. The result is that most people want the information or want to be entertained "now" as they look for instant gratification. Media content providers, to survive, are sensitive to these audience needs. One result is to use proven formulas such as portraying racial minorities as "villains." Here's a quote from a noted scholar that illustrates this point:

> It is an easy thing to do. It is the thing that is going to be most readily accepted by a large number of the audience. It is the same thing as throwing in sex and violence when an episode is slow.[20]

"It" is portraying racial minorities as villains.

Realistic Media Portrayals Are Balanced Portrayals

Realistic portrayals show a group in all possible facets of the human experience. This includes the good and the bad. For example, in portraying Hispanics, gangs may be part of the media reality, but so should Hispanics who are astronauts, schoolteachers, war heroes, and presidential candidates. Although Whites are also portrayed negatively, the general media landscape for them is predominantly positive or simply day-to-day living. The media should do the same for racial minorities.

Racists Process Information Differently

How we think and organize information about our environment affects how we think about race. There are differences in how much people can tolerate unfamiliar and uncertain events, objects, and other people and in our ability to make sense of complex information, our acceptance of change, and, in general, our ability to understand other people. Researchers who study these individual characteristics call them "cognitive style." Comparisons of people who score high in explicit and implicit tests of racism show some differences with people who score low. Racists, compared to nonracists, are generally intolerant of unfamiliarity and uncertainty (ambiguity). They prefer simple yes and no answers, are less open to alternative perspectives, and are less capable of making sense of complex information and of abstract reasoning. Also, they prefer stability to change, are less trusting of other people, less sensitive to other people, and less capable of identifying other people's behaviors and intentions. Some researchers call these differences in abilities "cognitive rigidity;" others call them "social conservatism." These differences distinguish between racists and nonracists and have consistently been confirmed in a number of scientific studies in the last decade.[21] These studies are typically surveys of adults. Other characteristics that might affect racial bias are controlled for statistically, such as education and age, so there is strong support that cognitive rigidity predicts racism.

In 2012, British researchers published a study that had begun over 20 years ago. They assessed the general intelligence of children in the United Kingdom when the children were 11 and 10 years old. They measured general intelligence with standard tests that tapped cognitive abilities such as verbal intelligence (similarities between words), nonverbal intelligence (similarities between shapes and symbols), "matrix abilities" (drawing missing aspects of shapes), digital recall (remembering digits from a series of numbers), word definitions (identifying the meaning of words), and word similarities (generating words that are semantically consistent with presented words). The children were interviewed again at age 30 (3,412 men, 3,658 women) and again at age 33 (4,267 men and 4,537 women). Social conservatism and racism were measured at ages 30 and 33.

The researchers defined social conservatism as "resistance to change and a desire to maintain existing social stratifications," as well as endorsement of socially conservative values such as "desire for law and order, punitive reactions toward wrongdoers, adherence to social conventions or traditions, and social control." To measure these values, survey respondents were asked to strongly agree, agree, disagree, strongly disagree, or express no opinion to statements such as "give lawbreakers stiffer sentences;" "schools should teach children to obey authority;" and "family life suffers if mum is working full-time." Racism was defined as negative feelings towards minority (non-White) groups in general. To control for other factors besides general intelligence and social conservatism that might affect racism, the researchers also measured parental socioeconomic status when the participants were children (social prestige of occupation) and personal socioeconomic status when they were adults (social prestige of occupation, level of education). Socioeconomic status and education were controlled for statistically so that their potential influence on racism would be accounted for, leaving only general intelligence and social conservatism as potential influences on racism. This was a well-planned study over time, tracking individuals from childhood to early adulthood and using standard measures validated in the field.[22]

The study showed that general intelligence at childhood predicted racism in adulthood. The lower the intelligence scores, the higher the racism scores; 62% of boys and 65% of girls who scored below the median of the intelligence test at age 10 showed above median levels of racism in adulthood, compared to 35% to 38% of the children who scored above the median in intelligence tests. The study also found that social conservatism and racism were significantly related in adulthood: The more socially conservative, the more racism expressed by the adult sample. General intelligence was significantly related to social conservatism in adulthood: The less intelligence, the more socially conservative.[23]

So, are racists dumb? This was the headline of a news story describing this study when it first was published.

No, not all racists are "dumb." I would caution against calling anyone "dumb" because the term is derogatory and really does not mean much. Intelligence tests, like most standard tests of mental reasoning, are what the tests measure, not whether a person is "dumb."

The UK researchers found that when controlling for the effects of social conservatism on racism, the effects of intelligence were not very strong. Therefore, intelligence does not have a direct effect on racism. However, there is a pretty strong indirect influence. Low intelligence leads to political conservatism, which leads to racism. Children who score low on intelligence tests grow up to be political conservatives. Political conservatives are more likely to be racists.

The results of this particular study, while provocative, should not be overread. They do show a link between low intelligence and racism. However, this link, while statistically significant, is generally modest when controlling for education and socioeconomic status; only about 6% of racism is explained by intelligence directly. Not all people who score low on intelligence tests are racist; not all social conservatives are racist. At the same time, the results of this study should not be dismissed. If we adopt a definition of intelligence as a cognitive style rather than as a biological predisposition, the link to racism, no matter how small, provides guidance on how education and exposure to different people and objects can teach people to think abstractly regardless of political or social ideology. Abstract thinking, the research suggests, is a key element of being open-minded, and therefore of being less likely to be racist.

Other research has suggested that abstract thinking is developed in childhood, a result of parent/caregiver interactions with the child and early education. Prompting the child to ask and answer questions about race, for example, can foster abstract thinking about race. Race to children is an abstract concept, so prompting them to think about racism requires abstract thinking.

Group Dynamics and Identity Explain Racism

Group memberships are crucial to our understanding of how racism develops. The groups we belong to are sources of our identity, who we are. They provide affirmation and support of self-worth. We belong to many groups and have several identities. These groups and identities perform a common function: They help us navigate through an uncertain environment. To organize our environment, we consciously or unconsciously categorize people into in-groups and out-groups. In-groups are the groups we identify with; we belong because of common interests and beliefs and because they support who we are. Some examples of in-groups are sports fan clubs, job or career organizations, hobby groups, political groups, nationality, and race. It's a natural thing to do. We seek others who are like us because it takes less effort to interact with them (disagreements, which are stressful, are minimized), and we need reinforcement for our identities (who we are) and self-worth. Identifying with and joining in-groups can be harmless. However, when we assign negative traits and behaviors to other groups (out-groups) and treat all their members in the same way based on these perceptions, then bias and prejudice result.

Racism occurs when other races are considered inferior out-groups and are feared by in-groups. Fear leads to racism. We don't fear all out-groups. For example, White nationalists (an in-group for some racists) may consider immigrants an out-group. They may not fear Norwegian immigrants, but they fear immigrants from Mexico, Africa, and Asia.[24]

Perceived Threats Lead to Fear; Fear Leads to Racism

We fear groups that we think threaten our in-group, and therefore our identity. Threats can be perceived to be "real"—that is, threatening the very existence of our in-group. Examples are threats to political and economic power, territorial boundaries, wealth, natural resources, and, in general, the existence of the in-group.[25] White supremacists, for example, fear that immigrants from non-White countries will "eliminate" the White race from the United States. Threats can also be perceived to be "symbolic"—that is, they will undermine the culture of an in-group, its values, beliefs, customs, language, and way of life. White supremacists believe that immigrants from countries they perceive to be "un-American" will dilute and eventually eliminate American culture, which to them is White culture.

A study in Texas, Florida, and Hawaii provides evidence that perceived threats lead to racism. The researchers asked college students about perceived realistic and symbolic threats from immigrants from

Mexico (Texas sample), Cuba (Florida sample), and Asia (Hawaii sample.) Realistic threats were crime, disease, drugs, job loss, and economic costs for health, education, and welfare. For example, survey respondents were asked to agree or disagree with, "Mexican immigrants are contributing to an increase in crime in the United States." Symbolic threats were perceived differences between an immigrant group and "American culture," such as "Mexican immigration is undermining American culture." The study also measured negative stereotyping of the immigrant groups (such as dishonest, unintelligent, clannish, lazy, not friendly) and negative feelings toward the immigrant group (hostility, dislike, inferiority, disdain.) Results from all three states consistently showed that perceived realistic and symbolic threats predicted negative stereotyping and negative racial feeling. In the Texas sample, perceived threats accounted for 72% of prejudice toward Mexican immigrants.[26]

Threats Are Inaccurate or Exaggerated

Most people, particularly racists, exaggerate the threats posed by out-groups, including immigrants. We develop these beliefs from isolated experiences, in-person or online conversations with like-minded people, and selective use of bits of information from the media. It takes an open mind and effort to evaluate the validity of perceived threats from information that is available from credible, nonbiased sources such as official government sources (for example, the U.S. Census Bureau).

chapter three

Who Is a Racist?

T hree men chase jogger Ahmaud Arbery in their pick-up trucks and corner him. One of the men shoots Mr. Arbery with a shotgun and says over his body, "F***ing n***er." The three men, who are White, are charged with murder. Their defense attorneys deny they are racists.[1]

Most Americans are not overt racists, but most of us have unconscious biases. Some estimates place the number of overt, White supremacy racists at 10% to 25% of adult Americans,[2] while unconscious racists are 80%.[3] These are rough estimates. Overt racists are identified by membership in White supremacist and other hate groups or by their ideologies, often revealed in social media posts. Implicit racists are identified from studies of the Implicit Association Test.

It's not easy to identify even an overt racist because words and actions included in the definition of racism can be rationalized as not having anything to do with race. A person might demonstrate behaviors and language that could be defined as racist yet deny being racist. Compounding the problem of identifying racists is the protection of speech and related actions by the First Amendment (a cost certainly justified by freedom of speech). Most racist speech and actions are protected, so a person demonstrating racism may claim their right to free expression. The exception to

First Amendment protection in the United States is "incitement to imminent lawless action or true threats ... a serious expression of an intent to commit an act of unlawful violence to an individual or group of individuals."[4] A person does not have to demonstrate criminal behavior to be racist. A person using hate speech, even if protected because it is not a "true threat," is a racist by definition in the United States and Europe. In the United States, hate speech "attacks a person or group on the basis of attributes such as race, religion, ethnic origin, national origin, sex, disability, sexual orientation, or gender identity."[5] Attacks are threats of physical or emotional harm, which may not meet the criminal standard of "imminent" or "true," and expressions of hostility. In Europe, hate speech is similarly defined as "all forms of expression which spread, incite, or promote or justify racial hatred, xenophobia, antisemitism, or other forms of hatred based on intolerance."[6] The U.S. and European definitions of hate speech are similar, identifying race a factor in being targeted and in specifying language that express hate. These expressions need not be criminal. A person, by using hate speech, is a racist by definition.

Hate Groups Are at Their Highest Numbers in the United States

Although they will deny it, hate groups are racist. Underlying their ideologies and actions is the belief that other races are inferior to their own and should be treated accordingly. Several civil rights organizations and the Federal Bureau of Investigation (FBI) in the United States have defined and identified hate groups. Their definitions include hate toward a number of groups, race being a primary target.

The Anti-Defamation League (ADL) defines a hate group as "an organization whose goal and activities are primarily or substantially based on a shared antipathy towards people of one or more different races, religions, ethnicities/nationalities/national origins, genders, and/or sexual identities."[7]

According to the Southern Poverty Law Center (SPLC), a hate group is "an organization that—based on its official statements or principles, the statements of its leaders or activities—has beliefs or practices that attack or malign an entire class of people."[8]

The FBI defines a hate group as an organization whose "primary purpose is to promote animosity, hostility, and malice against persons belonging to a race, religion, disability, sexual orientation, or ethnicity/national origin which differs from that of the members of the organization."[9]

According to these definitions, hate groups demean and vilify other groups by assigning negative traits and behaviors to them, labeling members of target groups as "inferior" because of group membership. Racial minorities are often a target, as illustrated in these hate groups identified by the Anti-Defamation League:[10]

- White supremacists subscribe to an ideology that includes one or more of the following beliefs: "1) White should have dominance over people of other backgrounds, especially where they may co-exist; 2) white people should live by themselves in a Whites-only society; 3) White people have their own culture that is superior to other cultures; 4) White people are genetically superior to other people; 5) the White race is in danger of extinction due to a rising 'flood' of non-Whites who are controlled and manipulated by Jews; and 6) imminent action is needed to 'save' the White race."[11] Traditional White supremacists include the Ku Klux Klan, the Council of Conservative Citizens, and the League of the South.[12] To illustrate hate and racist language used by White supremacists, David Duke, former Grand Wizard of the Ku Klux Klan in a recent tweet called for the "chasing down" of specific Black Americans.[13] Patrick Little, candidate for the U.S. Senate in 2018, claimed in Gab (a censorship-free alternative to Twitter), that ovens are a "means of preserving the Aryan race."[14]
- Alt Right, short for "alternative right," "consists of a loose network of racists and anti-Semites who reject mainstream conservatism in favor of politics that embrace implicit or explicit racism, anti-Semitism and White supremacy."[15]
- Christian Identity followers, according to the ADL, believe that people of European ancestry are descendants of the "Lost Tribes" of ancient Israel and are therefore the chosen people of God. They believe that "non-Whites were created

by God not when God made 'man' but when he created the 'beasts in the field;' that non-Whites are 'mud people.'"[16] Christian Identity followers should not be confused with Christian fundamentalists who strongly oppose their views.[17]

- Neo-Nazis, a main subgroup of White supremacists, "revere Adolf Hitler and Nazi Germany and sometimes try to adopt some Nazi principles to their own times and geographic locations."[18] (For example, neo-Nazi leader Billy Roper posted this tweet in response to immigrant families being separated in the U.S. Mexico border: "#KeepFamiliesTogether Deport them all, along with any who support them. With a catapult."[19])

- White Nationalists support White supremacy and White racial identity. They seek "to promote the interests of Whites exclusively, typically at the expense of people of other backgrounds."[20] James Allsup, a White nationalist leader, posted a photo of migrant children behind a fence with the caption, "They present it like it's a bad thing."[21]

Hate groups identified by the Anti-Defamation League, the Southern Poverty Law Center, and the FBI do not necessarily engage in criminal acts since many of their activities are protected by the First Amendment. However, given our definition of racism, we can identify many of their followers as racist.

Who are the followers of racist hate groups, such as White supremacists? Researchers have identified some personality traits that distinguish self-identified members of extremist hate and racist groups from the rest of the population. Typically, the research takes a sample of self-identified members of the hate group and a comparable sample of people who don't identify with the group. Members of both samples are then asked about their attitudes, beliefs, behaviors, and personality traits. One study compared self-proclaimed members of Alt-Right with people who did not identify with Alt Right.[22] Controlling for age, gender, education and other demographics, the study showed that Alt-Right identifiers were more likely than non-identifiers to report the following:

- Higher online aggression such as verbal abuse
- Higher levels of antisocial behaviors such as interpersonal aggression against others

- Lower levels of empathy (ability to imagine self in another person's situation)
- Higher levels of Machiavellian tendencies (willing to manipulate others for own gain)
- Higher levels of narcissism (inflated sense of self-importance)

According to other researchers, members of White supremacist groups in general are insecure, have felt "humiliated" or "insignificant" at school, in relationships, or in their communities and "society."[23] These insecurities lead White supremacists to seek validation of self-worth and "belonging" in their groups, to blame others (such as minority racial groups) for their own failings and disempowerment, and to consider themselves as superior to minority groups.[24]

According to researchers, some public statements by leaders, including the president, help explain the resurgence of White supremacy hate groups at an increase of 182% in White supremacist propaganda online posts between 2017 and 2018.[25] People attracted to White supremacist ideology blame other people (such as racial minorities) for their perceived disempowerment.[26] White supremacist groups provide them with a sense of belonging and a sense of significance.

White supremacists and members of other hate groups are at an extreme end of the racism spectrum and represent only a small percentage of the American population. The majority of Americans are not extreme racists. Most of us, however, may have unconscious biases that influence how we evaluate and interact with members of other races.

How Do I Know if I Have Explicit or Unconscious Racial Biases?

Research has shown that about 50% of Americans will reveal racial biases in a questionnaire, and about 80% will reveal unconscious biases in a computer-based test (the Implicit Association Test.) Race bias questionnaires are usually administered in surveys. The IAT is taken voluntarily and requires access to a computer.

Explicit Racism Can Be Measured

These questionnaires ask a respondent how they feel about different racial groups. Since they are often used in research such as surveys, most people are reluctant to openly express their real feelings and opinions. Even with this reluctance, recent surveys have shown that about 50% of American adults show some bias toward minority races. Most of the surveys ask White respondents about their feelings and opinions regarding Black Americans. These feelings and opinions are measured using scales, or a set of items, usually asking for agree/disagree responses. The items cluster in common themes indicative of bias against a racial group. A scale often used by researchers is the Modern Racism Scale (MRS). The scale measures White racism toward Blacks, although other racial minorities can be substituted for Blacks. According to items in this scale, a person who is biased against Blacks believes that racism against Blacks is a thing of the past; Blacks are too pushy and demanding of their rights; this pushiness results in unfair tactics; and the advances and gains Blacks have made are undeserved.[27] A biased person will object to laws and policies meant to mitigate racism against Blacks and other minorities, such as affirmative action. Most White supremacists, for example, strongly oppose affirmative action.

Here are some items in the Modern Racism Scale: Respondents are asked whether they strongly agree, agree, have no opinion, disagree, or strongly disagree with each item. Some items are supportive of Blacks; others are critical. Biased or racist people will agree or strongly agree with most of the anti-Black items and will disagree or strongly disagree with the pro-Black items.[28]

- Over the past 5 years, Blacks have gotten more economically than they deserve (anti).
- Over the past 5 years, the government and news media have shown more respect for Blacks than they deserve (anti).
- It is easy to understand the anger of Black people in America (pro).
- Discrimination against Blacks is no longer a problem in the United States (anti).
- Blacks are getting too demanding in their push for equal rights (anti).
- Blacks should not push themselves where they are not wanted (anti).

The Modern Racism Scale measures opinions that indicate bias against Blacks. Another scale that measures bias against any racial group (or any group) is the Bogardus Social Distance Scale.[29] This scale measures behaviors or social distance, as opposed to opinions, which are generally more accurate indicators of bias. The Bogardus Scale assumes that social distance—how far or near a person is willing to accept another person into their social space—is an indicator of prejudice. The closer the distance, the less prejudice, and, conversely, the greater the distance, the more prejudice. Racists will wish to keep their distance from members of other races; the more different in physical appearance and culture, the greater the distance. The Bogardus Scale first identifies the "target" group and then asks respondents whether they would accept a member of that group into one or more of these relationships. Answers are yes or no; the more yes answers, the less prejudice.

- As close relatives by marriage
- As close personal friends
- As neighbors in the same street
- As coworkers in the same occupation
- As citizens in their country
- As only visitors in their country
- Would exclude from their country

The Bogardus Social Distance Scale measures the level of acceptance of various racial and ethnic groups in the United States. Racists will generally express exclusionary distances for certain racial minority groups such as Blacks.

Implicit Racism Can Be Measured

The Modern Racism and Bogardus Social Distance scales ask directly about opinions and actions toward a racial group. Even if we answer the questions anonymously, we are aware which answers are "socially acceptable," that is, not racist. Therefore, these scales may be underestimating the extent of racism in any population. Most racism is implicit; that is, it is unconscious, unthinking, automatic and intuitional.[30] Implicit racism operates at an unconscious level; we are not even aware that we are acting or thinking as a racist. It is manifested impulsively and is activated automatically by the mere presence of the target person without conscious intention or awareness. Implicit racism, although unconscious, directs our evaluations of and actions toward the targeted person. Among the most talked about demonstration of unconscious racism is the "shoot or don't shoot" response. Research has shown that most people (even well-meaning people who do not want to be racist) unconsciously associate danger, violence, and weapons with dark skin.[31] There is also evidence from experimental studies that college student research participants will more frequently and more quickly "shoot," in a video game, unarmed Black men compared to unarmed White men.[32] I discuss other consequences of implicit biases in the next chapter.

Most of us have implicit biases as a result of socialization—the influence of parents, peers, media, and our environment. We may try to reject these biases consciously. However, they are often imbedded in our long-term memories and can direct actions without our conscious consent at any given moment when primed.

Implicit biases are measured by the Implicit Association Test (IAT) developed by two psychologists, Drs. Greenwald and Banaji, in the mid-80s.[33] Over 3 million people have taken the test in the United States and other countries. Most people who take the test do not want to be racist and do not think of themselves as racist. They take the test because they would like to control whatever implicit biases they might have so as not to act in a racist way. They also have a higher level of education than the general population. Among people taking the test are judges, lawyers, physicians, schoolteachers, university professors, college students, and, more recently, police officers.

The IAT measures how we unconsciously and automatically assign valence (positive or negative feelings) and traits or stereotypes to groups of people (such as races) or objects. Using a computer keyboard, the test-taker clicks on keys to associate traits or feelings with groups or objects on a computer screen. The speed with which an association is made is measured in milliseconds by the computer; the less time it takes, the stronger the association. About 80% of people taking the IAT show a racial bias, such as a more positive evaluation of light skin tone over darker skin tone. To take the test, and for a detailed discussion of results, go to https://implicit.harvard.edu/implicit/takeatest.html or search for "IAT Project Implicit."

Who, then, is a racist? We can start with members of extremist hate and racist groups who are explicitly and unabashedly racist.

Then we have the over 50% of Americans who reveal racist opinions and attitudes in survey questionnaires but who are not "hard-core racists" like the extremists. And finally there is the over 80% of Americans who have implicit racial biases but who would like to control these biases. So, it seems most of us are racist in one degree or another.[34] A positive note is that most of us would like to not be racist. And there are actually ways in which we can control our racism, discussed in the last chapter.

chapter four

Why Does Racism Matter?

Although racists are difficult to identify because of self-denial, racism is demonstrated in their actions, most visibly physical violence directed at innocent people because of the color of their skin. Racist acts are chronicled in stories told by victims and reported by media, in objective data collected by research and government and private organizations, and in controlled studies mostly in universities. The consequences of racism can be observed in everyday life, law enforcement, health care, employment, politics, and schools. Racism affects not only the physical and emotional well-being of victims but also their self-concepts and performance in tasks related to negative stereotypes.

Racial Profiling

Racist behaviors result from racial profiling, the unequal or discriminatory treatment of a person because of their perceived membership in a racial group. Often the discriminatory treatment is based on a subtle, covert, or unconscious evaluation of the group based on stereotypes. The resulting behavior is explicit, that is, can be observed or recorded. Although racial profiling can result in positive outcomes (such as an airline passenger being upgraded based on clues pointing to affluence and prestige), most racial profiles are based on negative evaluations and stereotypes, resulting in exclusion, discriminatory behaviors, or harsher punishment. People of color are often racially profiled based on negative stereotypes. Some stereotypes that direct racial profiling are as follows: Blacks are poor, uneducated, and violent and are gang members and criminals; Hispanics are "illegal" and are drug dealers and gang members; Asians are foreigners; and people of color, in general, are undesirable members of the community.[1] In most cases, racial profiling is practiced by members of the dominant group; in most communities in the United States, White Americans, older males in particular, are the dominant group.[2] Of course, not all older White American males are racist. In fact, many of them lead anti-racist initiatives.

Racial Profiling in Everyday Life

Racial profiling is demonstrated in many interactions on a daily basis, such as when people of color use public spaces. Consider these recent headlines from the *Huffington Post* and other online news sources:[3]

- "Ivy League Economist Suspected of Terrorism While Doing Math Aboard American Airlines Plane"
- "British Tourists Who 'Looked Middle Eastern' Caught Up in Terror Scare in Canada"
- "British Asian Man 'Victim of Racial Profiling' by US Border Officials"
- "White Man Calls Police on Black Mother and Child for Using Neighborhood Swimming Pool"
- "I Interviewed for Scientist Position, but I Was Asked About Terrorism Instead"
- "Kroger Manager Accused of Racial Profiling After Calling Cops on Black Teens Buying Snacks"
- "Massachusetts Attorney General Probes Racism Allegations Against Boston Museum"
- "Texas Police Tried to Arrest a Black Man in His Own Yard After Misidentifying Him"
- "Black Hotel Guest Making a Call in Lobby Accused of Loitering, Loses His Room"

In each of these reports, a person or persons were subjected to discriminatory actions based on preconceptions about race. The allegations proved to be wrong. These instances of racism were initially reported in social media and picked up by mainstream media. Many of the perpetrators were identified and ridiculed; some of the organizations apologized to the victims and instituted "anti-bias" workshops. These incidents of racism happen every day, all too often. These examples represent just a small sample.[4]

Shopping and Racial Profiling

Have you ever felt ignored or treated poorly in a store because the clerk perhaps thought you "did not belong" and could not afford the merchandise, or worse, were a shoplifter?

Some years ago, I went to a high-end (that is, expensive) furniture store in a lake town where we had a cabin. The store specialized in hand-crafted log furniture and decorative items. I was looking for a wooden bear. There was only one person in the store. I presumed he was the manager or owner. He was on the phone, so I did not bother him. He glanced at me and resumed his phone conversation. I waited 1, 2, 3 minutes. He was still on the phone, ignoring me. A middle-aged couple, yes they were White, entered the store. The manager ended his phone conversation and asked the couple (the man, actually), "How can I help you?" Of course I was angry. Did he ignore me because of my race? Or because I was in blue jeans, sandals, and an old sweatshirt? When the couple left without buying anything, I approached the manager, who still seemed disinterested, and told him that my wife and I had just bought a lakeside cabin as a vacation home (true) and that we wanted to furnish the whole house with his log furniture (not true). His demeanor immediately changed. He was friendly and showed furniture that I could custom order. I bought a bear from him, which he carried to my vehicle. Was he racist? I do not know. Quite often, store clerks consider people of color as unwanted customers or as shoplifters because they can't afford the merchandise. Consider this report from NBC News:

> A 19-year old college student is suing New York City and a luxury department store because he was handcuffed and locked in jail after buying a $350 designer belt. The college student, who has no prior arrests, told

NBCNewYork.com that he saved up from a part-time job to buy the belt, and that he wondered, as he was taken to a cell in handcuffs: "Why me? I guess because I'm a young black man, and you know, people do a credit card scam so they probably thought that I was one of them. They probably think that black people don't have money like that." According to the lawsuit, the checkout clerk asked to see the young man's identification when he was paying for the belt. After the sale went through and he left the store, he was approached by police about a block away, and asked 'how a young black man such as himself could afford to purchase an expensive belt.' The lawsuit stated that officers took the young man to the local precinct where he showed police his identification as well as his debit card and the receipt for the belt. Police still believed the young man's identification was fake, and called his bank, which verified it was his. The young man's attorney told a newspaper, "His only crime was being a young black man."[5]

Our young man's story is repeated many times by experiences of Black Americans every day. African Americans encounter discriminatory treatment while shopping, such as increased scrutiny by security personnel and lack of attention from salesclerks. Black shoppers are often viewed as "second-class citizens in retail markets."[6] In several studies, Black shoppers (confederates of researchers) were followed around and watched more often than comparable White shoppers. They waited longer to be acknowledged and attended to by sales staff. Blacks were 10 times more likely than Whites to report consumer profiling and discriminatory actions. Education and type of retail outlet did not make a difference. Racial profiling was observed and occurred in small stores, big box stores, and stores where expensive goods were sold and by low and highly educated Blacks.[7] A conclusion is that Blacks, regardless of education and the type of store they are shopping in, are generalized into a second-class consumer category and as unable to pay, likely seen as having criminal intent. It is unclear to what extent formal store policy directs profiling. It is clear that in most instances store personnel internalize what they perceive as the store's culture, leading to racial profiling, and are responding to consumers based on unconscious biases.

Another recent study in New York City provides evidence that racial profiling of Blacks while shopping continues. The study found that of 55 Blacks working in managerial and professional occupations, white-collar jobs, and blue-collar jobs, 80% recalled being racially profiled in apparel and high-end stores. Specific discrimination reported by Blacks interviewed included being perceived as a shoplifter or thief (59%) or as being poor (52%). Fifty-two percent reported that they were ignored by sales staff and were offered no service.[8]

Traffic Stops and Racial Profiling

Perhaps you have been stopped by a police officer when you were not breaking any laws and wondered why. Sometimes you get off with a warning; other times, a ticket and an unpleasant experience. I've had my share of traffic stops, a few my fault for sure, but others made me wonder. Was I stopped because I was breaking the law or was it because of my vehicle, the way I looked, the way I drove, or the neighborhood I was in?

I am zooming along a two-lane state highway, 5 miles over the posted speed limit on a sunny day, about 40 miles from home. My 9-year-old son is asleep in the front seat, tired after playing in a tennis tournament. I am wearing dark sunglasses. A state police cruiser going the opposite direction in the other lane slows down, flashes his lights, and turns his vehicle around. I pull over. The state trooper approaches my window. I see that he has unhooked the fastener to his firearm holster. I take off my shades.

"Do you know why I stopped you?" he asks, sounding irritated.

"Sorry officer, I don't know."

"Going a little too fast there," he says.

"Sorry officer, I lost track." (*Five miles over the speed limit, I thought*).

"Nice car. What is it?"

I tell him.

"This car yours?"

"Yes." (*Of course; to whom else might it belong?*)

"Mind if I look around?"

Now, what do I do? I ask myself. I vaguely remember that the law says search only with probable cause. What is probable cause? Probable cause for what? Why am I probable cause? Perhaps I got the law wrong. No big deal; I just want to get home. By this time, my son is awake. I can see the concern (fear?) in his eyes.

"Go right ahead," I tell the officer.

The officer looks through my son's tennis bag and our overnight bags. He asks for my driver's license, car registration, and proof of insurance. I ask his permission to retrieve the documents from the glove compartment, which I give to him. He tells me to stay put and goes back to his car.

The officer walks back to my car and hands me back the documents. This time, he is friendly and asks about the car. I tell him and point to the speedometer, saying that they really shouldn't put speedometers in street cars that read up to 160. He smiles, tells me to take it easy, and that he'll let me go with a warning this time.

Days, later, I asked an attorney friend, was I profiled? Did I respond correctly? He said I was likely profiled because of the car and how I looked. I acted "properly" (to avoid a confrontation), even if there might have been grounds to refuse the search. It's best, he said, to comply and be polite. The place for redress is in the courts if the encounter turned out badly.

I've followed my friend's advice since that encounter and rarely have had any trouble. But it's not always easy to be polite and compliant, particularly when blatant racial profiling is perceived by the person stopped and the police officer's behavior is confrontational.

According to national and state statistics, Blacks, Hispanics, and other racial minorities are stopped more often than their White counterparts. Police pull over more than 20 million motorists every year. The Stanford Open Policing Project analyzed 200 million records of traffic stops since 2015 and concluded that "significant racial disparities in policing" exist.[9] Although these disparities can be caused by factors other than racial profiling (such as driving behavior), some of the data point to racial bias. For example, officers stop Black drivers at higher rates than White drivers. Compared to White drivers, Black drivers are 20% and Hispanic drivers 30% more likely to get a ticket rather than a warning. And, Black and Hispanic drivers are twice as likely to be searched compared to White drivers.

Data from states such as California, North Carolina, and Washington[10] provide similar statistics. In Washington state, Black, Latino, Native American, and Pacific Islander drivers were stopped and searched at higher rates than White drivers.[11] However, state troopers were actually more likely to find drugs, weapons, and other illegal items when searching White drivers.[12]

Racial Bias in the Courtroom

Considerable research in law and the social sciences has analyzed whether defendants are treated equitably in the courtroom.[13] Most studies suggest that race is a factor. Blacks, in particular, receive different treatment than Whites. For example, judges in Connecticut set bail amounts that were 25% higher for Black defendants than for "similarly situated" (such as similar crimes) White defendants after controlling for 11 variables that might affect bail amount.[14] Federal judges imposed sentences on Black Americans that were 12% longer than sentences on Whites for comparable crimes.[15] Killers of White victims are more likely to be sentenced to death than are killers of Black victims, and Black defendants are more likely to receive the death penalty.[16]

Controlled laboratory studies provide explanations for the higher conviction rates for Blacks compared to Whites for similar offenses. One explanation is that jurors in mock trials judge ambiguous evidence to be more indicative of guilt when the alleged perpetrator has dark skin compared to when the perpetrator has light skin. As a consequence, mock jurors are also more likely to find dark-skinned alleged perpetrators guilty compared to light-skinned alleged perpetrators.[17]

Blacks compared to Whites are more likely to be misidentified as suspects.[18] In one study, White college students read a short newspaper story about a violent crime accompanied by a photo of either a Black or White suspect. After reading the story, the research participants were shown photographs of the suspects in the newspaper article and photos of Black and White men not shown in the news articles. Participants were then asked to indicate whether the man in each photo was the suspect in the news stories. The Black men who were not shown in the newspaper story were mistakenly identified as the suspect significantly more often than the White men not shown in the story, leading to the conclusion that Black men, in particular, are more likely to be misidentified as suspects.

Why are Blacks treated differently in the courtroom? Implicit racial biases and stereotypes are one explanation. Research has consistently shown an implicit preference for Whites over Blacks in the United States and an unconscious association of Blacks with violence and crime. Judges and jurors are just like the general population. Their unconscious biases influence actions and evaluations even if they don't realize this influence.[19]

Racial Bias in Decisions to Shoot

Are police officers more likely to shoot Blacks than Whites? Some evidence suggests that Blacks are five times more likely than Whites to be killed by police.[20] In 2015, 41% of all people killed in large cities by police officers were Black.[21] Blacks were 13% of the population.[22]

The discrepancy in Black and White fatalities can be explained to some extent by environmental factors. Most Black fatalities happen in predominantly Black neighborhoods and in high-crime areas. However, causal conclusions cannot be drawn from comparing these statistics because of the absence of strict controls. There may be other factors that explain the differences that are not readily apparent in comparing fatalities between neighborhoods. One such factor is racial bias or racism.

The effects of racial bias on the decision to shoot or don't shoot has been studied in controlled experiments for almost 2 decades. Understandably, the "shooting" scenarios are not real but are simulations of real-life situations. In the typical experiment, participants watch a series of neighborhood images on a computer screen. A person soon appears in the scene, typically male, holding an object. The person is clearly Black or White. Study participants are instructed to press a keyboard button labeled "Shoot" if the person on the screen is holding a gun or a button labeled "Don't Shoot" if the target is holding a harmless object such as a phone or wallet.[23] These studies have been done with White college students, community members, and police officers.

Results showing a racial bias have been consistent among the different study groups. College students, community members, and police officers "shot" (by pressing the "shoot" button) armed Black men more frequently than armed White men. They also did not shoot (by pressing the "don't shoot" button) an unarmed White man more quickly than an unarmed Black man. Also, study participants erroneously shot unarmed Blacks more often than unarmed Whites and more frequently did not shoot armed Whites than armed Blacks.

These results indicate that at first encounter in the context of the study White college students, community members, and police officers demonstrate a racial bias: They more quickly shot armed Blacks than armed Whites and more often shot unarmed Blacks than unarmed Whites.

However, in repeat encounters (repeating the simulations at least once), participants, particularly police officers, demonstrated significantly less racial bias. They made fewer errors in decisions to shoot or don't shoot, and racial differences were much lower than in initial encounters. These results suggest that training in evaluating the situational threats (suspect holding a weapon or harmless object), which are routine for police officers, and training in unconscious bias control can mitigate discriminatory actions in real-world shoot or don't shoot situations.[24] The internal mechanism leading to reduced error rates with training is "cognitive control." When made aware of our unconscious racial biases, most of us will make a conscious effort to disengage from behaviors based on those biases.

Why the racial bias in decisions to shoot or don't shoot? Unconscious stereotypes, which lead to bias, are "primed" or activated in the presence of individuals representing "target" groups, particularly in stressful and ambiguous situations where decisions have to be made in split seconds (such as the shoot or don't shoot scenarios). Studies have consistently shown that even with the best intentions to be unbiased, most White Americans (80% according to some estimates),[25] unconsciously associate Blacks, particularly men, with danger, crime, and violence. When activated, these stereotypes can direct our actions. People who more strongly hold these stereotypes, even implicitly, are more likely to demonstrate racial bias in the decision to shoot compared to people who believe these stereotypes less strongly.[26] These stereotypes are reinforced in our everyday vicarious interactions (such as in the media) with Blacks. For example, exposure to news focusing on Blacks as criminals reinforces the association of Blacks with crime and increases the bias to shoot Blacks.[27] Whites who are overt racists or who have strong unconscious racial biases will more likely be influenced by those biases as they interact with Blacks and other people of color compared to the average White person.

Race Supremacy Ideologies in Law Enforcement

Most police officers are not overt racists. However, like the rest of us, they have unconscious racial biases and stereotypes that can direct actions and decisions toward the targets of those biases. When those actions can have fatal consequences, such as in shoot or don't shoot decisions, bias control cannot be overemphasized. Bias control won't deter police officers who are White supremacists from killing or otherwise harming people of color. In the first place, they should not be allowed to be on the police force.

As far back as 2006, the FBI reported that "ghost skins"—members of neo-Nazi or other hate groups posing as members of "civilized society"—had joined police departments across the United States.

In 2016, the Plain View Project in Philadelphia identified more than 5,000 Facebook posts and comments by police officers in eight cities that included racist stereotypes, promotions of the Confederate flag, comparisions of Black Lives Matter to the Ku Klux Klan, jokes about extrajudicial executions, Muslim vilification, and encouraged violence against minorities. In 2019, the Center for Investigative Reporting reported that active-duty officers in more than 50 police departments across the United States were posting racist memes on Facebook. Also in 2019, ProPublica uncovered a group of 9,500 current and retired U.S. Custom and Border Protection officers posting xenophobic and White supremacist imagery on Facebook.[28]

Why are some police officers drawn to race supremacy ideologies? One study, working on the premise that people pursue careers that offer opportunities to express their inherent traits and preferences, found that compared to civilian populations police officers value conformity, social dominance, and power more and universalism, self-direction, and outgroup contact less. Also, police officers in general, compared to civilian populations, had stronger group orientation (us versus them) and placed greater value on hierarchical rank and organizational structure, power over others, and top-down management.[29] These are personality traits that other studies have shown to be correlated to racial bias.[30]

The vast majority of law enforcement officers are dedicated public servants (witness them kneeling and marching in support of people protesting George Floyd's killing). It's difficult to separate the good officers from the bad officers until it's too late. Some proposed solutions are not to hire the bad people in the first place and engage in continuous screening through an outside agency. Posts on social media can reveal support of racist ideology.[31] Racial bias, then, should be a litmus test for the recruitment and retention of law enforcement officers.

Racial Bias in Health Care

An overweight man walks into a doctor's office complaining of chest pains. Will he be treated differently depending on his race? Most of us would say no or hope that that the answer is no. But the data show otherwise. Racial minorities, particularly Blacks, generally receive lower health care quality than Whites even after controlling for income, education, access to insurance, age, healthy behaviors, and health condition.[32]

- A study of 400 hospitals showed that Black patients with heart disease received older, cheaper, and more conservative treatments than comparable White patients. They were also less likely to receive coronary bypass operations and angiographs, and were discharged earlier from the hospital at a stage when discharge was inappropriate.[33]
- Black patients receive fewer referrals for cardiovascular procedures than comparable White patients.[34]
- Physicians prescribe less pain medication to Black patients compared to White patients.
- Black women are three to four times more likely than White women to die from pregnancy-related causes.[35]

These studies show that Black Americans are not receiving the same quality of health care that their White counterparts receive even when factors other than race that might affect health care are controlled for. If income, education, access to insurance, age, lifestyle, and health condition do not account for discriminatory treatment, then what does? Numerous studies in the past decade suggest that unconscious biases of doctors influence their treatment of patients. These studies show that doctors are just like the rest of us. They have implicit biases and stereotypes of people based on race. They do not intentionally treat patients differently based on race, but implicit negative associations influence their decisions.[36]

Physicians do not express explicit racial biases. However, measures of implicit bias show they are no different from you and me. In one study of 2,500 doctors who took the Implicit Association Test, White, Asian and Hispanic doctors showed a significant preference—measured by the association of positive words with a photograph of a Black or White person—for Whites over Blacks. Black doctors showed no preferences.[37] The stereotypes most commonly associated with Blacks were that they were less cooperative than Whites and were less likely to follow medical procedures.

In several studies, implicit biases influenced the treatment doctors prescribed to patients and their communication with patients. Doctors with implicit biases prescribed less treatment for Black patients compared to White patients.[38] Doctors high in implicit bias spent less time with their Black patients and were less supportive compared to doctors low in implicit bias. Also, doctors with high implicit bias dominated conversations more with Black patients than did doctors with low implicit bias and were less receptive to questions. Black patients picked up on these racial bias cues. They trusted high implicit biased doctors less than low implicit biased doctors, had less confidence in them, and rated their quality of care poorer.[39]

The evidence clearly demonstrates that physician implicit biases lead to differential interactions and treatment of Black patients, who receive less effective treatments than White patients. The good news is that when doctors are made aware of these biases, they work to control biases so that they do not make discriminatory decisions or take discriminatory actions. While typical diversity programs focusing on the importance of "diversity" are not effective in motivating doctors to control biases, workshops that emphasize motivation, awareness, and effects of biases are effective.[40]

Racial Bias in Schools

Decades of research have shown that minority school children, including Blacks, Hispanics and Native Americans, do not perform as well in academic measures of school success and are more often punished compared to White students. These gaps for the most part persist even when controlling for home and neighborhood environments like poverty, school policies, and school procedures.[41]

The gaps between minority and White students begin in preschool. Blacks, particularly Black male preschoolers, are 3.6 times more likely to receive one or more suspensions compared to White male preschoolers.[42] In one study, Black children made up only 19% of preschool enrollments but were 47% of preschoolers suspended one or more times.[43] Other studies have found similar disparities in K–12 students.[44] Black students are more likely than White students to be expelled or suspended. Black students are punished more than White students for similar offenses, even when controlling for classroom achievement, parental education and income, self-reported behaviors, and teacher-reported behaviors.[45]

Disparities also exist in academic programs and performance. Black students are 54% less likely than White students to be recommended for gifted education programs even when their standardized test scores are equal. Race of the teacher was a factor. Black students were three times more likely to be referred to gifted programs if their teacher was Black rather than White.[46] National data reveal substantial gaps in mathematics and reading scores between Black and Hispanic school children and their White peers even when controlling for home and neighborhood factors such as poverty rates and school quality. In mathematics, fourth-grade Black students perform below their White peers by about the equivalent of 18 months of school. By grade 8, the gap is 32 months. In reading, the gap for fourth-grade Black students compared to their White peers is 23 months and is 34 months for 8th graders. The gaps between Hispanic and White students are similar, although not as large.[47] The disparities in academic achievement of children are demonstrated by on-time high school graduation rates, which are 82% for Asian students, 78% for White students, 57% for Hispanic students, 57% for Black students, and 53% for American Indian students.[48]

Approximately 50% of the disparities in student achievement can be attributed to "between school" differences in school quality, teacher demographics (percentage of racial minorities), and neighborhood poverty.[49] The other 50% can be explained by within school differences such as school policies and procedures and teacher interactions with students and expectations. Expectations and interactions, in turn, are affected by implicit race biases. Teachers are just like the general population taking IATs, and, as such, we can expect that 70% to 80% of White teachers will have unconscious biases favoring Whites over Blacks and other students of color. Recent data estimate that about 80% of K–12 teachers are White.[50] In IAT results for the general public, Black respondents generally show no preference for Blacks or Whites or show a moderate preference for Blacks. White respondents generally express a preference for Whites.[51] Teachers show similar results as the general population, which explains why in classrooms with Black teachers Black children generally perform just as well as White children and are punished at the same rates. The disparities observed in achievement and punishment are observed in classrooms with White teachers.[52]

Consider this anecdote related by Dr. Tracey Benson:

> Question: "Can you talk a little about some of the ways unconscious bias is impacting students in schools today?"
>
> Dr. Benson: "I have a lot of specific examples. One, being a student of color who attended a predominantly white school for the majority of my life, I've experienced a very keen sense and a keen eye for one, being the receiver on the receiving end of biases from either teachers or professors, and also as a principal, I've seen it happen in school. Let me give you an example. There was a teacher, I think it was my second year as principal, and I hired a teacher at our school, a younger teacher to teach one of our classes. I went into her classroom and I observed her for efficacy in terms of her instructional style, her pedagogy, her classroom management, and things of that sort. But while I was observing the classroom, I had noticed that out of the 25 students she had in her classroom, she had five rows, and at the very end row were sitting all four black students. The only four black students that were in that class were sitting in that row.

As the teacher was teaching, I was noting down which students participated, which students asked questions, just to see the amount of teacher talk time and student talk time. While I was marking down the marks on my page, I noticed that none of the black students were participating. Not only were they not participating, but they weren't being called on. There are no cold calls, they weren't raising their hands, there was no active participation in the classroom. Then I started watching what the teacher was doing. As I watched the teacher, I noticed that she was standing almost cutting them off. She was standing in a place in the classroom with her back turned away that she was actually not able to see that row at all because her overhead projector, and she was writing on her overhead projector to demonstrate math problems, she was cutting out that half of the room.

I thought to myself that this could be a reason why these students aren't participating on this end because the teacher doesn't even see them. I wondered how long this has been going on. And so, I made the decision, and this was a young white female teacher, to talk with the teacher about it, because it's a teacher that I had hired. In sort of calibrating whether or not to have a conversation with the teacher, I also have to think of myself as a black male educator. I don't want to make them feel like I'm accusing them of being racist. This is something that I see in the classroom and you probably don't even know that you are doing it. Luckily at our post observation conference, I let her know what was happening and I showed her the drawing.

I said, 'Did you notice that your body faces away from these students, the black and brown students?' She said, 'I'd never noticed that before.' I was like, 'Well, why don't you try changing your position and see what happens as a result, and see if these students will participate a little bit more.' She asked me to come back in two days, which I did. I came back in two days for another observation. I could only stay 30 minutes, but I noticed that she's, one, changed her position, and two, she goes actively cold calling on the students more, just by being made aware that something could possibly be going on in the classroom, it increases students' level of participation. That's one of many, many ways that unconscious bias plays out in the classroom in a way that a teacher just simply doesn't know until someone points it out."[53]

Dr. Benson's story illustrates how unconscious biases might affect teacher-student interactions in the classroom. His interpretation of the lack of interaction between a White teacher and her Black students as being possibly caused by implicit biases that the teacher may not even be aware of is supported by controlled studies where other possible causes of differential treatment of students of color are accounted for. Here are some results of these studies:

- Instructors with greater implicit pro-White/anti-Black biases as measured by the Implicit Association Test predicted lower performance on the material being taught for Black students but not for White students. This suggests that biased instructors, when told that their teaching material was for Black students, predicted lower performance. When they were told that the same material was for White students, they predicted higher performance. High-biased instructors teaching Black students also gave less clear and engaging lessons to Black students compared to low-biased instructors.[54]
- College students given a story about a 10-year-old child with minor challenging behavior rated a Black child to be less innocent and more guilty compared to a White child for the same offense. They also estimated that the Black children were 4.5 years older than they really were, while estimates of the age of White children were more accurate.[55]
- School teachers are more likely to recommend severe punishment and report they are "more troubled" when minor school violations (such as classroom disturbance) are attributed to children with stereotypically Black names compared to children with stereotypically White names. Black children are more likely to be punished than White children for the same offenses.[56]
- A major predictor of a teacher's intent to expel a preschooler is the degree to which a child is perceived to be a danger to

other children. Danger is often associated with race and age. Black children, even if they are the same age as their White classmates, are often perceived to be older.[57]

- Preschool teachers and staff observed Black boys more closely than White children and Black girls even when engaged in normal (nonchallenging) behaviors. According to the authors of the study, teachers and staff may have unconscious expectations that Black boys will more likely engage in challenging behaviors and therefore need to be watched more closely.[58]

The evidence indicates that unconscious racial biases affect teachers' behaviors in the classroom. Biased teachers engage children of color less and are more likely to evaluate the behaviors of racial minority children, particularly Blacks, as challenging; they also are more likely to support harsher punishment, particularly for Black boys. Teachers, for the most part, don't consciously engage in discriminatory behaviors and evaluations. Like the rest of us, their unconscious racial biases can trigger automatic responses even without their knowing it.

Racial Bias in Politics

President Barack Obama and Racial Bias

The presidential campaign and election of Barack Obama as president triggered hundreds of racial hate incidents recorded by the FBI and various Watchdog groups such as the Southern Poverty Law Center;[59] many of these incidents did not meet the standard of imminent harm or violence, but some did. The threats to candidate Obama led the Secret Service to place Obama under its protection earlier than any presidential candidate in May 2007, 18 months before the 2008 presidential election. That protection continued through President Obama's terms and will continue through his lifetime,[60] an exception to 1994 legislation stating that presidents elected to office after January 1, 1997 would no longer receive lifetime Secret Service protection. The concern over Mr. Obama's safety as a prominent Black candidate, as the first U.S. African American president and president emeritus, was prompted by direct threats and "chatter" in White supremacist and other hate websites, as well as by implicit or covert hate language and images in mainstream media. Legal and social science scholars as well as watchdog groups like the Southern Poverty Law Center and the Anti-Defamation League have chronicled many of the threats using racist language and images directed at Obama.[61] Some of these acts were sponsored by known hate and White supremacist groups; others were done by "ordinary" citizens as individuals. Here are some examples:

- In 2008 before the elections, several White supremacists threatened to shoot candidate Obama, planning to go on a killing spree in a predominantly Black school, "beheading 14 Blacks" and assassinating Obama. They were arrested by law enforcement officers.
- After President Obama's election, some citizens in Maine rallied against his victory, using imagery of Black figures hung by nooses from trees. Also in Maine, a sign in a convenience store invited customers to join a betting pool on when Mr. Obama would be assassinated, with a parting message, "Let's hope we have a winner." In a New Jersey town, crosses were burned in the yards of Obama supporters. At North Carolina State University, someone spray painted the university's free expression tunnel: "Kill that niXXXX" and "Shoot Obama." In Milwaukee, Wisconsin, someone distributed a poster of Mr. Obama with a bullet going through his head. A University of Texas member of the football team (who was later expelled from the team) posted on his Facebook page, "All the hunters gather up, we have a niXXXX in the White House." In an Idaho town, a sign on a tree offered a "free public hanging" of Mr. Obama. In another Idaho town, some second and third graders on a school bus chanted "Assassinate Obama."

According to one estimate[62] more than 2,000 new members were recruited by a popular White supremacist group the day after Obama's election. It's clear from the language and threats that racism is the underlying ideology driving the haters. While most people, even members of hate groups, deny being racists, these behaviors demonstrate explicit racism. Most reasonable people would find these expressions and demonstrations of hate abhorrent. The concern is how much harm racists and haters can inflict on the rest of us, not to mention on the "targets" of their hate. A related concern is how racist language and images can "trigger" hateful and racist acts, not only by avowed racists but also by the about 80% of American adults who have implicit racial biases. Racist language and images, when repeatedly reported in mainstream media, may lead the general public to believe that overt support for racism is more prevalent than it really is and may provide hate groups with the publicity that they seek. Of course, the media should report racist actions such as killings. However, racist imagery and language are another matter. Their currency in our daily discourse or conversations can lead to tragic consequences. Whether intended or unintended, these expressions, no matter how subtle, can lead to devaluing the attacked groups and to violence toward them. There is a substantial body of scientific research that shows how primes—such as language and images in the media and our daily conversations—can activate latent racial biases and direct our evaluations of and interactions with targeted racial minority groups.

An example of racist imagery directed at then President Obama is the February 18, 2009 political cartoon in the *New York Post* that showed two policemen standing above a chimpanzee shot dead by one of the officers. Three bullet holes are shown on the chimpanzee's chest; blood stains are visible on the grass beneath the corpse. Above the head of one of the officers is a bubble that reads "They'll have to find someone else to write the next stimulus bill." Although the *Post*'s editor in chief defended the cartoon as a "clear parody of a news event—the killing of a violent chimpanzee in Connecticut" —critics, including newspaper editors and civil rights leaders, saw the cartoon as a racist attack on President Obama, the primary author of the economic stimulus bill. The *Huffington Post* reported that "at the most benign, the cartoon suggests that the stimulus bill was so bad, monkeys may as well have written it. Most provocatively, it compares the President to a rabid chimp."[63] The Reverend Al Sharpton called the cartoon "troubling at best given the historic racist attacks of Blacks as being synonymous with monkeys."[64] The president of the National Association of Black Journalists said, "To compare the nation's first Black commander in chief to a dead chimpanzee is nothing short of racist drivel."[65] A Virginia state senator called the cartoon "a throwback to the days when Black men were lynched."[66] Racist imagery like this cartoon, particularly in mainstream media, can prime latent racial biases and reinforce explicit racism, leading to evaluations and actions that dehumanize the targeted individuals and their races. This particular cartoon, according to one analysis, increased the threat to President Obama's life by extreme racists.[67]

President Donald Trump and Racism

The election of President Donald Trump in 2016 prompted several scientific studies analyzing his victory. Many studies identified the characteristics of voters who supported and opposed Trump. One of those characteristics is racism or negative bias toward non-White races. A key finding is that racial bias and related personality traits were key factors in support for Trump, although not the only factors.

In the typical study, random samples selected to be representative of the adult American population are surveyed on the internet. The sample sizes range from a few hundred to several thousand. In the 2016 campaign, respondents were asked about support for either Hillary Clinton or Donald Trump, strength of support, political ideology and affiliation, questions that measure racial bias, and behaviors and personality traits shown by previous research to be related to racism and conservative political ideologies. Examples of these variables are authoritarianism (deference to authority, resistance to new experiences, a rigid hierarchical view of the world); social dominance orientation (preference for dominance of lower status groups); and lack of contact with dissimilar groups such as other races. Other variables that might explain support for or opposition to Trump are also measured. Examples are perceptions of relative economic deprivation (lack of social mobility, feeling "left behind"), strength of party affiliation, ideology (conservative/liberal), education, and other demographics. The relationship between support for Trump and racial bias is analyzed statistically, controlling for all the other variables. As we can expect, the strongest predictors for support of Donald Trump over Hillary Clinton were party affiliation and political ideology. However, racial bias was also a strong and consistent predictor of support for Trump even when controlling for ideology and political party affiliation. People who expressed bias against Blacks and other racial minorities were more likely to support Trump over Clinton.[68] Among leaning Republicans, anti-immigrant sentiments predicted a Trump vote.

Among strong Republicans, racist resentment predicted Trump support.[69] Other variables predicting Trump support were sexism (prejudiced attitudes toward women), authoritarianism, social dominance orientation, and lack of contact with other races.[70] In most of the studies, perceptions of relative economic deprivation were weak predictors of Trump support.

These studies consistently show that racism was a factor in Trump support in the 2016 elections. Many of these studies show that up to 25% of the probability that a person would support Trump was predicted by racism, racial resentment, or anti-immigrant sentiment. Other factors such as party affiliation and political ideology were generally stronger predictors. Not all, or even most, Trump supporters were racists. However, many of them were.

To measure racism, survey respondents in these studies were asked standard questions that have been validated in decades of research. Several surveys measured "color-blind racism" (denial that racism exists) by asking respondents to strongly agree, agree, disagree, or strongly disagree with the following statements. They can also say that they have "no opinion:"

- White people in the United States have certain advantages because of the color of their skin.
- Racial problems in the United States are rare, isolated situations.
- I am angry that racism exists.

Anti-immigrant attitudes were measured in one study by asking respondents whether immigration in general had a positive or negative impact on the economy, cultural life, and life in general in the United States.

The measures in these studies have their weaknesses. Most people are not willing to express their true sentiments, particularly with regard to racism and immigration. Estimates of racism and anti-immigration attitudes are most likely less than what they really are. This underestimation does not invalidate the common finding that racism was a factor in support for Trump in 2016.

Trump Supporters Respond to Racial Cues

If at least some of the support for Trump in 2016 was influenced by racial bias, how would Trump supporters evaluate a policy that is cued to a racial minority? An internet study provides evidence that simply on the basis of a racial minority cue such as a photograph, the response would be negative.[71] In this study, over 700 White adults were selected from a national sample. They were asked if they supported candidate Trump or candidate Clinton. Half of the Trump supporters saw a photo of a home with a "foreclosed" sign in front, accompanied by a photo of a Black man. The other half of Trump supporters saw the same photo but with a White man. A text introducing the photos read, "Recently, there have been proposals to help people who are struggling with their mortgages." The study participants were then asked whether they supported the mortgage program, whether such mortgage help would make them angry, and the extent to which they blamed the homeowner for the foreclosure. The men in the photo were matched for age and attractiveness. The only difference was that one was Black, the other White. Study participants were assigned randomly to the Black or White photo conditions to equalize any other factors (such as strength of support for Trump or Clinton). Results show that Trump supporters who saw the poster with a Black man indicated stronger opposition to mortgage assistance, had more anger toward assistance, and blamed the homeowner more compared to Trump supporters who saw the poster with a White man. The racial cue, a photo of a Black or White man, influenced how Trump supporters evaluated a public policy, emotional reaction, and the assignment of blame.

The study showed the opposite results when repeated with Clinton supporters. The Black cue (photo) compared to the White cue resulted in greater support for the mortgage policy and less anger and less tendency to blame the homeowner.

These results provide evidence that implicit racial biases, which previous research has shown to be more likely found among 2016 Trump supporters compared to Clinton supporters, elicited negative evaluations of a public policy when prompted by a racial cue, a photo of a Black man.

Did Words From Candidate Trump Matter?

A 2016 study of over 1,000 non-Latino White adults suggest that words from Trump denigrating Mexicans influenced Trump supporters to express negative attitudes toward Mexicans.[72] Half of the sample respondents, randomly selected, read this quote (among a number of other quotes to disguise the purpose of the study): "When Mexico sends its people, they're not sending their best. They're sending people that have lots of problems. ... They're bringing drugs. They're bringing crime. They're rapists. And some, I assume, are good people."[73]

The other half of respondents, randomly selected, read other quotes, not including the quote about Mexicans. After reading the quotes, respondents in both groups were asked, "In a few words, please let us know what comes to mind when you think of the following groups." The groups were Blacks, Mexicans, Whites, politicians, the middle class, and millennials. The group of interest was Mexicans. Other groups were included to disguise the purpose of the study. Respondents typed in their comments in a small text box in a computer screen. Comments were then analyzed by trained coders who classified the comments as negative or positive. Study participants who read the Trump quote about Mexicans said more derogatory and offensive remarks about Mexicans compared to study respondents who did not read the Trump quote. These negative comments about Mexicans included stereotypes and negative feelings.

We cannot conclude from this study that the Trump quote caused people to be more prejudiced against Mexicans because we don't know if those prejudices already existed. However, it's clear that the negative characterization of Mexicans in the Trump quote led to greater expression of prejudices, causing people to be more willing to express what may have been unconscious biases toward the targeted group.

Racism, Voting, and Opinions on Issues

The effects of racism extend beyond physical threats to candidate and President Barack Obama. Racism also affects how we vote and our opinions on issues. Large-scale surveys in the 2008 elections showed that implicit prejudice against Blacks predicted a vote against Barack Obama. In one study, individuals who scored high on the race Implicit Association Test (strong preference for Whites over Blacks) were 42.5% less likely to vote for Obama, controlling for education, political party affiliation, and ideology.[74] High Black bias scores on the IAT also predicted opposition to the Obama health care proposal. Supporting the survey evidence is experimental evidence that racial bias predicted opposition to the health care proposal. In a 2009 study, half of the study participants, randomly selected to control for demographics that might influence their opinions, read a summary of the health care proposal, which was attributed to President Obama. The other half of the participants read an identical summary attributed to former president Bill Clinton. Study participants high in Black racial bias as measured by the IAT evaluated the health care proposal negatively and opposed it when the proposal was attributed to Obama. They were less likely to oppose the proposal when it was attributed to Clinton, leading to the researchers' conclusion that "Obama's race—and not just the political or ideological character of his policies—underlies the relationship between prejudice and opposition to his health care reform plan."[75]

Racial bias is based on negative stereotypes, which influence opinions on race-coded issues. These issues don't explicitly identify race but implicitly connect negative stereotypes to support for or opposition to one side. Examples of race-coded issues are immigration, affirmative action, and welfare. National surveys have shown that the strongest predictor of opposition to welfare programs is the stereotype that Black Americans are lazy, followed by the belief that poor people are lazy, and by opposition to government control in general. Negative stereotypes were the most powerful predictors of opposition to government welfare programs even when education, party identification, and political ideology were controlled. Control variables had minimal effects on opposition to welfare. Other studies have shown that stereotypes of Black Americans as "lazy," "less intelligent," and "prefer to be on welfare" predicted opposition to affirmative action programs. Negative stereotypes of Hispanic (Spanish-speaking) immigrants as "poor," "unintelligent," "dependent on government assistance," and "violent" led to beliefs that immigration would lead to unemployment, lower quality of schools, and higher levels of crime. The evidence, then, suggests racial and stereotype biases influence opinions on political and race-coded issues.[76]

Racial Bias in Employment

Does racial bias affect how we evaluate applicants for jobs? It's against the law to explicitly discriminate based on race. But implicit biases can direct our evaluations prior to employment, such as decisions on whom to call back or interview. Studies in the United States and Europe have demonstrated that prospective employers discriminate on the basis of applicant race. In some of these studies, employers associate names with racial groups that are the objects of their implicit biases and make discriminatory decisions—deciding who to call back or interview—based on these associations. These decisions are made in favor of mainstream candidates, Whites in the United States and Swedish in one European study, even when the resumes submitted are identical. Here are examples of two studies supporting the conclusion that racial biases influence employment decisions.

Bertrand and Mullainathan sent out 5,000 resumes in response to more than 1,300 employment ads in Chicago and Boston.[77] The ads were for a wide range of jobs including sales, administrative support, clerical, customer service, and office and management positions. Half of the resumes were higher quality, highlighting qualifications such as experience; the other half were lower quality, with fewer qualifications and gaps in employment history. In half of the resumes, the applicant had a typical-sounding Black American name such as Lakisha Washington or Jamal Jones; in the other half, the resumes had a typically White American names such as Emily Walsh or Greg Baker. The researchers selected distinctively Black American and White American names from birth certificates in Massachusetts. They pretested the names in Chicago to confirm that the names they selected were African American or White American.

Results of the study showed that applicants with White names needed to send 10 resumes to get one callback, whereas applicants with African American names needed to send 15 resumes, a difference of 50%. Whites with higher-quality resumes received nearly 30% more callbacks compared to Whites with lower-quality resumes. For Blacks, there was no difference in number of callbacks between higher- and lower-quality resumes. These results suggest that employers made decisions based on race. Black applicants received 50% less callbacks than White applicants with identical resumes. The only difference in applicants was their race, as signaled by their names. Resume quality made a difference for Whites but did not matter for Blacks.

Similar results—showing racial bias against a minority group, this time Muslims—are shown in a study in Sweden.[78] A sample of employers took an Arab-Muslim Implicit Association test to measure implicit biases against Muslims. After the test, half of the sample read a resume from an applicant with an Arab name. The other half read a resume from an applicant with a Swedish name. The employers were then asked how likely they would interview the applicant. Employers who had at least a moderate negative implicit bias against Arab Muslims (56% of employers) were less likely to interview applicants with Arab Muslim names, such as Moham-med or Ali, compared to applicants with Swedish names. Among employers with little or no bias against Muslims the difference was not significant.

These studies provide evidence that implicit racial biases influence evaluations of job applicants even when racial cues are provided only by a name. Names are primes that elicit automatic reactions based on biases stored in long-term memory. Discriminatory decisions on whom to call back or interview are implicit and done without careful evaluation of information provided by identical resumes. Driving these automatic responses are stored and unconscious feel-ings toward targeted groups and implicit stereotypes. For Blacks, the stereotypes most likely activated are "lazy" and "violent." For Muslims, the likely stereotypes activated are "can't be trusted" and "terrorist." These stereotypes override the objective information in job resumes, leading to the conclusion that racial bias is the determining factor.

Racial Bias and Social Interactions

Do racial biases affect how we interact with people from other races? A related question is "How do our implicit and explicit biases affect our evaluations, judgments we make, of social interactions that we observe and that involve the targets of our biases?" For example, will our biases lead us to call a shove by a Black man an aggressive act while calling the same behavior a friendly nudge when done by a White man? The evidence from several studies suggests that racial biases indeed lead to less pleasant social interactions and to negative evaluations of observed behaviors by targeted groups.

In one study, White undergraduate college students took a Black-White implicit bias test. They then participated in a mock experiment with either a Black or White graduate student who gave instructions and answered questions. The graduate student "experimenters" had previously been rated by another group of students to be equal in attractiveness and interpersonal communication skills. The only difference was their race. The interactions of the student partici-pants with the Black or White experimenters, randomly assigned, were videotaped and rated by another group of trained coders as to whether the interactions were pleasant, positive, or negative using verbal and nonverbal cues validated in previous studies. Results show that White students with implicit negative Black biases had negative interactions, as rated by the coders, with the Black experimenter but not with the White experimenter. With the Black experimenter, biased White college students spoke less, asked fewer questions, smiled less, made fewer extemporaneous social comments (small talk), made more speech errors, and generally demonstrated negative body language.[79]

Another study shows that Germans with strong implicit biases against Turks (an immigrant group) evaluated ambiguous social behaviors by Turks negatively.[80] They evaluated the same behaviors to be significantly less negative when attributed to Germans. The study participants, who were all Germans, took a Turkish-German Implicit Association Test for anti-Turkish bias. They then read a brief report about a young man spending an evening at a dance club with friends. Half of the study participants, randomly selected, read the report with a photo of a Turkish-looking man, identi-fying him as the young man in the report; the other participants read the same report with a photo of a German-looking man. The photos were evaluated in pretests for equivalence of attractiveness and age. After reading the report with the accompanying photos, the research participants rated the young man's behavior on eight adjectives meant to measure positive or negative behaviors. The ratings were on a five-point scale, from 1 (not true) to 5 (true). The adjectives were objectionable, brash, cheeky, obtrusive, insensitive, obstinate, arrogant, and bigheaded. The results show that the German research participants rated the behavior at the dance club to be more negative when attributed to the Turk compared to the same behavior when attributed to the German. This difference in evaluations was greatest when the research participants had strong unconscious biases against Turks. They rated the behavior of the Turkish young man most negatively.

In the same study, research participants read four hypothetical vignettes with a photo of a young Turkish man or a photo of a young German man. Participants then were asked how the young man (Turkish or German) would act. In these vignettes A is either a Turkish or German young man as identified by a photo:

1. "One evening, A is walking along a quiet street. There is no one on the street except an old man walking a few meters in front of A. Close to the street lamp, the old man's wallet falls out of his pocket without him noticing it. How likely is it that A grabs the wallet and does not return it the old man?"

2. "A is at the train station and waits for the train to come. On arrival of the train, a big crowd emerges and a man hits A strongly with his suitcase. How likely do you think it is that A will get enraged in response to this event?"

3. "A few days ago, A was surprised to meet an old friend from high school. They immediately arranged a meeting at his friend's place. Now A is at his friend's place when he is asked by his friend whether he would like to smoke marijuana. How likely do you think it is that A accepts the offer?"

4. "One cold winter evening A is on his way back home from a party. It's about midnight and he is a bit drunk. On the way to his car, he considers whether to walk two kilometers to his home or to drive with his car. How likely do you think it is that A drives even though he is drunk?"[81]

Results show that implicit biases influenced how study participants rated anticipated behaviors in the vignettes depending on the race of the actor. Germans with strong unconscious biases toward Turks rated the actor to be more likely to engage in negative behaviors (such as driving home drunk) when he was Turkish rather than

German. The vignettes were identical; the only difference was the race, German or Turkish, of the actor.

These two studies are among many that provide evidence of the influence of racial bias in our day-to-day interactions with targeted races. When we have racial biases, these interactions are uncomfortable, cold, confrontational, and unlikely to lead to mutual understanding and respect. It's therefore not surprising that biased people avoid interactions with people from other races. What's more, racial biases influence how we interpret observed behaviors. Ambiguous behaviors are perceived to be more negative—contradicting social norms—when attributed to the targets of racism compared to when attributed to the mainstream race. Negative responses to targeted races are more evident in people who have strong biases and are less evident among people with weak and moderate biases.

The Coronavirus and Anti-Asian Bias

"Go back to where you came from. We don't want your sickness." The words came out of nowhere as I was checking out the tofu at a Walmart. I looked back at a White woman, in her 40s I would guess, slightly obese, eyes glaring at me, a toddler holding on to her hand. I slid my mask to uncover my mouth. "God bless you too," I said. "Stay well, stay safe." Perplexed, she was about to say something, then slowly walked away, her child turning his head to look at me with the hint of a smile. This experience is not unusual as the Coronavirus takes its toll on all of us. From news reports: An Asian American child is pushed off a bike by a bystander at a park. The owners of a Chinese restaurant in Yakima, Washington, found windows broken and a message spray-painted on a wall: "Take the corona back, you chink." A movie poster for *Mulan* is defaced in Pasadena, California, white mask spray painted over Mulan's mouth with the words, "Toxic, Made in Wuhan." In London, a young man from Singapore is punched and kicked by four men; one said, "We don't want your coronavirus in our country." An Asian American family is stabbed, including two children, at a Sam's Club in Texas.

The nonprofit Stop AAPI Hate has catalogued more than 1,000 reports of Coronavirus hate incidents against Asians in the United States in a 1-week period, March 19–25. According to a nationwide poll by the Center for Public Integrity, more than 30% of Americans have witnessed someone blaming Asian people for the Coronavirus pandemic; 60% of Asian Americans in the poll say they have witnessed anti-Asian hate. At the time of the survey, 95% of Americans were in quarantine.[82]

Why are Asian Americans, and Asians in general, being blamed for the pandemic? And why are they the targets of hateful actions?

All Asians Are Chinese

The first explanation is that the coronavirus did indeed originate in Wuhan, China, and, more importantly, most Americans do not make distinctions between the Chinese government, Chinese people, the different ethnicities included in "Asian," and Asian American. By physical features, therefore, anybody who looks "Asian" is responsible for spreading the virus and is a foreigner not to be trusted. According to the Pew Research Center, two thirds of Americans have an unfavorable view of China. For most Americans, it's easy to transfer the mistrust of China to anyone who looks Chinese and blame them for the virus.[83]

The American intelligence community agrees with the scientific community that the virus is not man-made or genetically modified. Also, the overwhelming infections of the virus in the United States came from Europe, not China. Before President Trump blocked travel from Europe on March 11, 2020, nearly 2 million travelers arrived in the United States from Italy and other European countries during February. Entry to the United States of any foreign nationals who had traveled to China was blocked by President Trump effective February 2, after China had imposed its own restrictions. Regardless, to most Americans, China—and by extension the Chinese people—are to blame for the pandemic. For their part, the Chinese Foreign Ministry was reported by CNN to have promoted on Twitter a conspiracy theory that the virus had originated in the United States and was brought to China by the U.S. military.[84]

Asians as the Other

In times of stress and uncertainty, it's human nature to deflect threats by blaming an "other." Asian Americans are a convenient "other" for mainstream White Americans. They look different, eat "weird" things, live in filthy and disease-infested "China towns," and are simply "different" from Americans. To most of the world an American is a White American. As I travel abroad, I am often asked where I'm from. I say, the United States, and I am American. The next question is, "Where are you really from?" a question I am often asked also in the United States. In the Middle East, Europe, and Asia, I am not American. My immigrant friends from the Philippines, who have lived in the United States as citizens for decades, refer to Americans as "puti" or White. They believe that they will never be Americans or accepted as Americans. They will never be White.

Many White Americans do in fact believe that Asians will never be Americans. Several decades of research in implicit biases indicate that Asian Americans are perceived by even well-meaning White Americans as "foreign."

Historical Racism Against Asians

Racism against Asians is rooted in U.S. history ever since Asians immigrated to the United States in the 1800s. Asians were good enough to be laborers—farm workers and railroad workers—but not good enough to be Americans. The Page Act of 1875 and the Chinese Exclusion Act of 1882 barred more Chinese laborers from entering the United States after the first groups of immigrants.[85]

Deep-seated racism toward Asians gradually transported from explicit to implicit biases in the United States as social and political norms changed with the civil rights movement in the 1960s. Implicit biases toward Asians are activated by primes or cues in the environment. In the current pandemic crisis, any mention or image associating the Coronavirus with China (for example, when the virus is called the "Chinese" virus) activates subconscious racism toward Asians.

The Coronavirus Pandemic Has Been Politicized

According to Politico, the National Republican Senatorial Committee distributed to Republican political strategists in April a report from a political consulting firm that detailed how campaigns should respond when asked about failures in the Trump administration's response to the pandemic. The report advised, "Don't defend Trump, other than the China travel ban—attack China."[86] A memo accompanying the 57-page report suggested three points of attack: China caused the virus pandemic by covering it up; Democrats are soft on China; Republicans will stand up to China.[87]

In the weeks to follow, President Trump publicly blamed China for the pandemic. He also said on Twitter and other public platforms that possible retaliation from the United States is justified; some TV networks are "Chinese puppets;" the World Health Organization took Chinese claims at face value. A Republican advertisement said, "Communist China hid their outbreak from the world, silenced their doctors, shut down investigations and blamed America."[88] Another political ad featured former governor and U.S. ambassador to China Gary Locke in an attack against presumed Democratic presidential candidate Joe Biden. The ad appeared to imply Locke is a Chinese official and not American. Locke, who is a second-generation American, told the *Atlantic,* "Asian Americans—whether you're second, third or fourth generation—will always be viewed as foreigners. We don't say that about second or third generation Irish Americans or Polish Americans. No one would even think to include them in a picture when you're talking about foreign government officials."[89]

Regardless of whether China is to blame for the pandemic, the vilification of China by some American leaders reinforces a social norm that says it is acceptable to publicly show displeasure toward Asian people. In this environment, displeasure can easily lead to acts of racism.

Stereotype Threat

A consequence of racism is the assignment of negative stereotypes to targeted races. These stereotypes—most of which have no basis in reality—direct our evaluations of and actions toward people based on their perceived race. Stereotypes affect self-efficacy and stereotype-related behaviors of persons who are targeted. This effect is "stereotype threat," sometimes referred to as the "self-fulling prophecy of stereotypes."

A premise of the stereotype threat concept is that persons targeted because of their perceived group (such as race) internalize the negative stereotypes, feel inadequate, and have lower expectations of themselves.[90] Dr. Claude Steele defines stereotype threat as "being at risk of confirming a negative stereotype about one's group."[91] The threat of confirming the stereotype arouses fear, stress, excessive performance monitoring, and self-consciousness, all of which result in poor performance on the task related to the stereotype.

Stereotype threat can be experienced by members of any group for whom a negative social stereotype exists. To affect performance, the stereotype should be specific enough so that it can be linked to a task related to the stereotype. Take the stereotype that Blacks are "not intelligent" in the classroom. This stereotype will be a threat when Blacks take a test that is presented to them as an important indicator of intellectual ability. When made aware of the stereotype, explicitly or implicitly, Blacks will consider it as a threat and will perform poorly on tasks related to the stereotype such as taking a test. Stereotype awareness comes from information in the media, other people, and cues or primes in the environment. Simply taking a test presented as a measure of "intelligence" can trigger the stereotype among Blacks that they are not academically qualified. Or a person in authority such as a teacher may explicitly tell their students that "Black students do not generally do well on this test." Awareness of the stereotype threat leads to poor performance and therefore confirms the stereotype even when it is not true, as is often the case.

Stereotype threat explains why Blacks, regardless of academic ability, may not perform well in standardized tests. In one study,[92] Black and White college students at a prominent university were given a test from the Graduate Record Examination (required by most universities for admission to graduate school). Half of the students, randomly assigned, were told that the test was a valid measure of intellectual ability (stereotype threat for Black students), while the other half were told that the test was for a laboratory study and that it had nothing to do with intellectual ability (no stereotype threat). Black students scored lower on the test compared to White students when the test was presented as a valid indicator of intellectual ability. There was no difference in test scores between Black and White students when the test was presented as a laboratory exercise. Stereotype threat was activated for Black students by presenting the test as a valid measure of intellectual ability. They performed more poorly compared to when the test was introduced as a laboratory exercise. Similar results are reported by numerous studies, providing evidence that stereotypes indeed can be self-fulfilling prophesies. Similar results have been reported for the stereotype that women "are not good at math." Stereotype threat leads members of targeted groups to confirm the stereotype even when they do not believe the stereotype.

Several interventions can mitigate the self-fulfilling prophecy of stereotype threat. A victim can summon another identity when performing the task—for example, college student rather than Black or a woman. Cues linking the task to the negative stereotype can be removed. A teacher administering the test can avoid mentioning race or gender. A teacher can also affirm self-worth of their students by emphasizing that they can do well on the test. The media can present more balanced portrayals of minorities so that not only negative portrayals are emphasized.

Stereotype threat is another harmful effect of racism. The ultimate solution is to deemphasize negative stereotyping of minorities in popular culture and public discourse.

chapter five

Addressing Racism

The hundreds of thousands of protesters who marched to demand an end to racial injustice in the aftermath of George Floyd's killing in May 2020 knew how to address racism. They were young, Black, Brown, and White, men, women, gay, lesbian, transgender. They were united in their sacrifice to bring about change.

Addressing racism means we—armchair protesters who share the same ideals—support our friends, brothers and sisters, and sons and daughters who have brought attention to the problem. What will motivate us to take action? And what action might that be? A first step is to reinforce our will to control racism in our subconscious psyches.

Not everyone can reduce their racial biases. Hard-core racists such as members of hate groups who explicitly proclaim their racism will not change. They are not candidates for bias reduction interventions. People most likely to reduce their biases are those who are prejudiced but don't realize it and who are interested in reducing biases. Close to 80% of Americans fall into this category. They have implicit racial biases that they are not aware of and they want to reduce or control their biases.[1] A smaller percentage—about 50%—express explicit racial biases but also are interested in controlling their biases.[2] Therefore, a large majority of

Americans are potentially interested in reducing and controlling their racism.

Most prejudice and racism reduction strategies require individual effort and motivation. For the most part, the strategies are voluntary and can be carried out without intervention from an outside authority. Other strategies depend on interventions from institutions like the media, schools, and government.[3]

Individual Strategies

Priming Motivation

My results on the Implicit Association Test show that I have a slight bias for Whites over Blacks and for lighter skin over darker skin. I do not want these biases to influence how I evaluate people and my actions toward people of darker skin. Priming this motivation—using the realization that I am biased as self-motivation—is the first step. I should realize and accept that I have biases. I took a test, so I know I have biases, but not everyone will want to take the Implicit Association Test. An alternative to taking the test is introspection. Thinking about instances when I have treated people differently because of their race or any other group membership can make me realize that I have implicit biases. We all have these experiences but usually don't think about them unless motivated to do so. Dr. Patricia Devine and her colleagues at the University of Wisconsin-Madison have developed an effective bias reduction workshop that primes motivation by asking workshop participants to write down instances where they may have demonstrated implicit biases.[4]

Here is a college student's story:

> Before spring break I was riding the bus and an older black gentleman sat in the seat next to me. I was about to sit closer to the wall but then realized that this was a stereotypical response and stayed where I was. I had to go get a drug test for my new job. While I was in the clinic a black woman walked up to the desk and the receptionist assumed she was there for a drug test also. I thought that was stereotyping on her part and I was right. The woman was there because she was injured at work.[5]

I use a similar strategy to make my college students in a Communication and Prejudice class realize that most people, including themselves, have implicit biases. At the beginning of the semester, I ask them to write about an experience in which they were the "perpetrators" of prejudice toward a person because of group membership. I also ask them to relate experiences in which they have been the victims of prejudice. The class is about 70% White; the rest are Blacks, Hispanics, Asians, and a few Middle Easterners. Most White students write about being perpetrators; most ethnic minority students write about being victims. Some of the experiences related by White students as perpetrators reveal, by their own admission, implicit biases, because most profess that they are not biased (a common research finding is that college students are less likely than the general population to be explicitly biased). Here are some common experiences:

- Assuming a Black student is an "affirmative action"
- Assuming a Black male student is an athlete
- Assuming a Hispanic student is an illegal immigrant
- Assuming an Asian student is international
- Moving to the other side of the street when a Black man is walking toward them

My students realize that these evaluations and related behaviors may be driven by unconscious biases. After writing the essays, many are interested in taking the Implicit Association Test.

The motivation to reduce prejudice can be generated internally or externally. I can be internally motivated if I am made to believe that most people who don't want to be biased are actually biased without knowing it, that bias is inconsistent with my values, and that controlling my biases is the "right thing to do." I can accept these beliefs by simply reading a short news article or essay or, more subtly, by asking myself questions such as "Is being nonprejudiced important to me?" and "Can I freely decide to be a nonprejudiced person?" The news story or essay and answers to the questions are reminders that I should do something to control my biases and that I am doing so of my own free will and not being forced to do so.

External motivations are primed by peer pressure, laws, or policies. I can be told by my employer or by my peers that I should not be prejudiced because I am expected by my friends, community, and society to be nonprejudiced, that discriminatory acts are against the law, and that I may be punished for certain discriminatory behaviors. I may be forced to take a bias reduction workshop. The motivation sources are external. I may believe in bias reduction, but at the same time I feel that bias reduction is something I should do because I am expected to be nonbiased.

Studies have shown that external motivations are generally not effective in reducing racism and other biases. People simply don't want to be told what to do and may resent the loss of autonomy or free will. On the other hand, internal motivations can reduce explicit and implicit biases, even after only one session. In studies, college students are randomly assigned either to an internal motivation condition or an external motivation condition. Each group reads an essay or answers a questionnaire priming internal or external motivations. Students who are primed with internal motivations reduce their explicit and implicit biases; externally motivated students show little reduction.[6]

Enhancing Accountability and Egalitarian Goals

I can reduce my unconscious biases by holding myself accountable for my prejudicial, including racist, behaviors. In controlled studies, college students who write down instances in which they had showed prejudice and the reasons for their behaviors subsequently showed less prejudice. Likewise, I can enhance accountability for my actions by recalling instances where I had behaved as a racist and attempt to explain them. I will not have problems recalling racist incidents but will probably have a difficult time explaining them except to admit that my behavior was driven by unconscious biases. This self-introspection will motivate me to regulate my behavior.

Most Americans believe that all people should be treated equally. Egalitarian goals are embedded in the constitution and, in theory, are American values. I can regulate my racial biases if I remind myself of these values and am mindful of them when I interact with people from other races. In a laboratory experiment, college students were primed to the egalitarian value by listing their own and American values. Typically, equality and freedom showed up in their lists. The students then imagined past experiences in which they had behaved toward African American men unfairly. Students participating in this exercise subsequently showed less biased stereotyping of African American men.[7]

Inducing Empathy by Eliciting Emotions

Empathy, or the ability to identify with others' feelings, can be an effective inhibitor of behaviors driven by implicit biases. Particularly effective are "perspective-taking" interventions, which encourage the individual to experience how victims of bias feel. Empathy can be activated by writing down or imagining instances where bias was demonstrated (such as racial profiling) from the perspective of the victim; imagining how victims feel when reading about or observing (as in media reports) incidents of bias and racism; and focusing on personal emotions when reading about or observing racist incidents. Studies show that these strategies can reduce racist and biased behaviors.[8]

Enhancing Value Consistency

Most people strive for consistency in our beliefs, values, and actions. I want my actions to be driven by my values. If I believe in the egalitarian principle, then I should treat all people the same. Inconsistency is uncomfortable, leads to stress, and will motivate me to change either my values or behaviors. So, first, I should remember or be made aware of my values. Then I should be mindful of my behaviors so that I can monitor them. I can make myself aware of my values simply by reminding myself of the values that are important to me and why they are important. Most likely, equality and freedom will be on my list. I can also look for demonstrations and reinforcement of my values, particularly equality, in traditional and social media. Studies show that we can regulate our biases when we accept equality as a value and when we accept that our behaviors should be consistent with equality.[9]

Personal Contact

The personal contact principle says that simple contact between groups can improve intergroup relations, including reducing implicit racism by reducing negative stereotyping. Personal contact allows us to "individuate," to see others as individuals rather than as members of a group such as a race, and to observe others in a wide range of behaviors. Personal contact provides information that could negate strict categorization from stereotyping. For personal contact to be optimally effective in reducing implicit racism, several conditions should be met. These conditions are equal status of the interacting individuals, cooperation to achieve common goals and shared goals, support by leadership in an organization, and minimal competition. Simple contact can be effective and is better than no contact at all. However, for optimal bias reduction, one or more of these conditions should be present.

Personal contact is most effective when voluntary, such as in schools and neighborhoods and at social events and work. Even mandatory contact can reduce prejudice. Studies show that prejudiced White adults assigned to Black coworkers to complete a project, minority and White college students assigned to dorm rooms, and racially mixed groups in an outdoor activity resulted in a reduction of prejudice.[10]

Here is an example of personal contact between a racist group and the target of their racism.

Can NAACP-KKK Meeting Reduce Prejudice?

The Associated Press reported that a representative of the Wyoming chapter of the NAACP and a Ku Klux Klan organizer met secretly in a hotel in Casper, Wyoming, under tight security.[11] According to the Southern Poverty Law Center, the meeting was a first. The Klan organizer paid $50 to join the NAACP. He said he joined the organization so he could receive the group's newsletters and some insight into its views. According to the NAACP representative, "It's about opening dialogue with a group that claims they're trying to reform themselves from violence. They're trying to shed their violent skin, but it seems they're just changing the packaging."

Extended and Vicarious Contact

Most of us have limited opportunities to interact in meaningful ways with people from other races. We like to stay in our comfort zones with people just like us so that we don't have to worry about how to act or talk and whether we are offending anyone. This self-isolation makes it more difficult to understand our biases, to individuate people who are not like us, and to break down stereotypes. An alternative to personal contact, which can effectively reduce racial biases, is extended and vicarious contact.

We extend contact with members of other races by observing interactions in television and the movies, by reading, and by engaging in conversations with others who have had direct contact. We can reduce implicit racial biases when the interactions are balanced, when not predominantly negative or positive, and, as in direct contact, when cooperation is demonstrated.[12]

The principles of personal contact can be applied to law enforcement. Anecdotal evidence (such as the Camden, New Jersey, police department) indicates that confrontations between police officers and citizens are significantly reduced when police officers interact with citizens in their communities, in social and civic events, and in daily activities not associated with crime.

Mental Imagery

The potential of imagined interpersonal contact as a prejudice reduction intervention is based on research indicating that mental imagery can elicit similar neurological, emotional, and behavioral responses associated with direct experience.[13] Mental imagery can be effective in reducing racial biases when the imagined interactions are friendly, pleasant, and rewarding. In one study, non-Muslim college students spent 2 minutes imagining themselves meeting a Muslim person for the first time, engaging in conversation that is relaxed, comfortable, and positive. After imagining Muslims, the students listed the ways in which the interaction was positive. They then took explicit and implicit tests of bias against Muslims. Compared to students who simply imagined Muslims without instructions that the interaction should be positive, and to students who did not imagine Muslims, students who imagined Muslims positively expressed less implicit and explicit biases toward Muslims. To be effective, mental imagery should be an interaction (members of both groups should participate) and be positive.[14]

Mediated Interventions to Reduce Racism

The prejudice reduction interventions I have discussed require proactive and self-initiated strategies. Other strategies require a medium or institution (an organization) to deliver the intervention. These mediated interventions are usually initiated by a mass medium (such as television, newspapers, social media). They can also be delivered by professional organizations (such as the Associated Press, the Asian American Journalists Association, the National Association of Black Journalists, the National Association of Hispanic Journalists, the Native American Journalists Association), private nonprofits (the Southern Poverty Law Center, the Anti-Defamation League), and private foundations (the Bill and Melinda Gates Foundation, the Knight Foundation, the Kellogg Foundation, the Ford Foundation). Interventions are delivered to large audiences via traditional media or the internet. Because audiences will not necessarily seek out interventions, audience participation is reactive (reacting to a message that we seek out or stumble on) rather than proactive (seeking out the intervention). Mediated interventions are less likely to be successful compared to individual and personal contact strategies. Potentially, much larger audiences can be reached and affected by mediated interventions.

Narratives

If prejudice arises out of ignorance, knowledge can be an antidote. We gain knowledge from stories we hear or read in the media, from friends, and from the internet. The media in particular can be effective instruments of bias reduction if they tell stories about racial minorities that are accurate and that are balanced portrayals of their life experiences—the good, the bad, accomplishments and failures, resilience, avoiding stereotypes, and considering minorities as individuals rather than having the group define the individual. We know from decades of research that traditional media, including those using internet platforms, have done a better job of accurate, balanced, and realistic portrayals of White Americans than of racial minority Americans, although there has been some improvement in the past decade.[15] Numerous studies have shown that narratives with the following elements can reduce prejudice:[16]

- Coverage of discrimination against racial minorities, particularly if written in the first person and if the story describes how the victims felt.

- Descriptions of positive interactions between in-groups and out-groups, such as between members of different races. These interactions could demonstrate cooperation, friendships, and shared experiences. This strategy is particularly effective with children.

- Emphasis in news and entertainment on celebrating and respecting (rather than simply tolerating) cultural differences. This strategy favors a "multiculturism" over a "color-blind" approach.[17] A color-blind theme proposes that social categories like race be disregarded and everyone treated as an individual, Proponents suggest that color-blindness assures equitable treatment. On the other hand, multiculturalism proposes that group differences and memberships should be acknowledged, celebrated, and respected. Cultural differences should not be erased in favor of a dominant culture. It's possible for groups to retain cultural norms and values while embracing a political national identity (such as allegiance to the U.S. Constitution). By respecting and understanding differences, the cultural and intellectual lives of all are enriched. Studies in the United States support the conclusion that multiculturism can reduce racial biases. In one study, students who read an essay promoting multiculturalism showed less explicit and implicit biases after reading the essay compared to students who read an essay promoting color-blindness. Applied to the media, news and entertainment content emphasizing and celebrating cultural differences generates positive intergroup attitudes and reduces racial bias, while contents that diminish or devalue these differences may reinforce prejudice. In New Zealand, for example, the Maori culture and language are celebrated and taught in schools and the media. Most universities have names in English and Maori.

- Exemplars: Counter-stereotypical exemplars in media news and entertainment can reduce implicit biases, including racism. Exemplars are individuals representing a group. Counter-stereotypical exemplars demonstrate positive traits and behaviors that disconfirm negative stereotypes. Take the negative stereotypes of Black men as violent and criminal. A gang member committing a violent crime confirms the stereotypes. A young man working with an after-school youth group disconfirms the stereotype. Other counter stereotypes are a Black woman professor or scientist, a Hispanic man or woman running for president, and a Muslim American receiving the Purple Heart for service in Afghanistan.

Positive exemplars in the media can reduce implicit biases because they provide information that can alert people to their unconscious negative stereotypes and motivate them to correct those stereotypes. There is evidence that the most effective strategy is to portray racial minorities in the same manner that the White majority is portrayed—realistic portrayals of everyday life, balanced for good and bad. Even with significant improvements in the past several years, media news and entertainment disproportionately portray racial minorities negatively, conforming to negative stereotypes, while portrayals of Whites are more balanced. Given this imbalance, increased counter-stereotypical depictions of minorities provide a reminder that not all members of a racial minority group are "bad" and not all members of the White majority are "good." Studies with college students have shown that exemplars were most effective in reducing biases when positive exemplars of a racial minority group were paired with negative exemplars of a mainstream group. In one study, students randomly saw photos of admired Black and disliked White individuals. They were asked to identify the person in the photos. Other students saw photos of only admired Black individuals or only admired Whites. A control group did not see any photos. Admired Blacks identified through pretesting included Martin Luther King, Jr., Jesse Jackson, and Michael Jordan. Disliked Whites, also identified through pretesting, included Timothy McVeigh, Charles Manson, and Al Capone. Students who saw admired Blacks and disliked Whites showed the least implicit biases toward Blacks compared to the other groups. The study was repeated with age-related exemplars (young and old) with similar results. Pairing admired "old" people with disliked "young" people reduced biases toward the elderly.[18]

Even with significant improvement in the past decade, portrayals in the media of racial minorities disproportionately confirm negative stereotypes, while portrayals of Whites are more balanced. Balanced and realistic portrayals of minorities will result in more positive exemplars, which will provide reminders to balance our mental pictures of them.

Media Interventions

Media groups and institutions can play a major role in reducing racial bias. A key to successful interventions is media content that highlights positive group interactions, counter-stereotypical exemplars, and narratives depicting stigmatized groups realistically. No matter how well designed the contents are, they won't be effective unless they reach the intended audiences. The media, because of reach, can be effective conduits of contents developed primarily in laboratory studies.

Support from media producers is not lacking. They provide guidelines for nonbiased marginalized groups. Here are some examples.

The Associated Press (AP) revised its style guide in 2013 to guide how "immigrants" is to be used in news reports. According to the new guidelines, "illegal" should not be used to describe people, as in "illegal immigrants," but be used to describe the actions people take. The AP policy shifts away from labeling people and toward describing behavior, as in, for example, "people diagnosed with schizophrenia" instead of "schizophrenics." The policy calls for detail in describing people who are in the United States without documentation required by law. For example, did they enter the country illegally, and from where? By crossing the border or overstaying a visa? What nationality?[19]

The AP policy calls for the abolition of labels—stereotypes—in its reporting and to describe behaviors instead. Similar guidelines on how to cover diverse groups are provided by minority journalism organizations such as the Asian American Journalists Association, the National Association of Black Journalists, the National Association of Hispanic Journalists, and the Native American Journalists

Association. Open to all professional and student journalists, these associations have developed style guides on how to cover racial minorities fairly and accurately to avoid stereotyping, An example is *ALL-AMERICAN: How to Cover Asian America*. The book gives pointers on how to cover Asian Americans with accuracy. It includes chapters on terminology to use and avoid in referring to Asian Americans to avoid biased stereotyping. Here are some examples about terminology:[20]

- "American: A citizen, native-born or naturalized, of the United States of America; not a synonym for White."
- "Asian American: Form the noun without the hyphen, as in 'French Canadian,' to denote current group membership."
- "Asian Gangs: *Caution:* Better to specify the country or ethnicity, such as Vietnamese or Chinese or Filipino gangs if relevant and the relevance can be explained satisfactorily."
- "Asiatic: *Avoid.* A 19th Century adjective typically used in pseudo-scientific European treatises assuming the superiority of the White race."
- "China Doll: *Caution.* A figurine, usually porcelain, but when used metaphorically, or as a comparison the implied image of female submission demeans women of Chinese heritage."
- Chinaman: *Avoid.* A slur, often applied to anyone of Asian heritage. A term from the 19th century, specifically for the poorly paid Chinese workers who risked their lives building the American transcontinental railroad, as in 'Chinaman's chance,' meaning no chance at all."

Narratives to Reduce Bias

Writers write what they know. Knowledge leads to narratives that are accurate and balanced. To tell stories that can reduce bias, writers, editors, and producers not only need the knowledge, but also the empathy to imagine what it's like to live as a member of a stigmatized group. Membership in the group leads to knowledge and empathy. That's why it's important to have minority representation in the media. For nonmembers, research and personal contact can provide knowledge and empathy.

The Aboriginal Peoples Television Network (APTN) of Canada is a good example of television providing accurate and balanced stories about marginalized groups. APTN's mission is to "air and produce programs made by, for and about Aboriginal Peoples."[21] Available to about 10 million Canadians, APTN produces and distributes documentaries, news magazines, dramas, entertainment specials, children's series, movies, sports events, and educational programs about Aboriginal peoples for a national audience. Its programming is about 56% English, 28% Aboriginal languages, and 16% French. APTN's staff is over 75% Aboriginal peoples.

APTN's model of programming for ethnic minorities can be found in other countries as well. During a recent trip to New Zealand, I was introduced to television programs that taught and demonstrated Maori culture to a national audience. Outside of television, I learned that Maori culture was valued and respected.

In the United States, the television documentary *The Native Americans* produced nearly 3 decades ago portrayed the history of Native Americans from their own perspective. Native Americans participated in the production as writers, producers, and consultants.[22]

A Concluding Note

After doing the research for this book, I have concluded that we—humans across the world—are all racist in varying degrees, from extreme haters like neo-Nazis, White supremacists, and the Ku Klux Klan to people who have moderate to slight implicit racial biases. If you are reading this book, you are probably in the "moderate to slight bias" category like me. Another conclusion I have reached is that racism cannot be eliminated. Biases favoring one race over another, no matter how wrong, have deep roots in the human mind and heart, given the human proclivity for protecting "one's own" and lifetimes of exposure to a culture of racism.

The good news is that most of us would like to understand and control our implicit biases. It's also reassuring that, in theory, most human institutions and governments proclaim they support egalitarian values. Ideally, these values are demonstrated in institutional policies, laws, and practice. These efforts will be successful only if change—bias control—is initiated and practiced. When people change, institutions will follow.

Change comes with individual motivation. Many of the strategies to control biases begin with the individual and can be accomplished only with self-motivation. These strategies require effort. This effort can be more manageable with a supportive environment. And that's where the media—traditional and digital—come in. We are inundated with information, some credible, others lies. From this mass of information, primes stick out that catch our attention—words, images, pictures, symbols, signs, people. Primes that support a culture of respect for others who are not like us go a long way toward supporting our own efforts at controlling racial biases. You and I can be such primes.

I have attempted to provide information from published social science research that might help us understand the beast in the room. There are many public and media misperceptions about racism—what it means, how it affects others, and how to reduce and control it. There is also a large amount of science on these topics, objective and verified information that unfortunately is mostly buried in academic journals not easily accessed. Hopefully, I have brought some of this information to you.

I conclude by echoing the advice of President Obama: organize, protest, speak loudly, and vote in local, state, and national elections. I would add: vote the unrepentant racists out. We know who they are.

References

Preface

1 *Newsweek*. (2020, May 3). Nike releases "Don't Do It" ad addressing racism in America. www.newsweek.com>2020/05/307/ nike-releases-dont-do-it-ad

2 Costs, R., Min Kim, S., & Dawsey, J. (2020, June 1). Trump calls governors "weak," urges them to use force against unruly protests. *Washington Post*. msn.com/en-us/news/politics/trump-calls-governors-weak-urges-them-to-use-force-against-unruly-protests

3 Axios.com/john-lewis-end-violence-george-floyd-protests; Culver, J., & Hauck, G. (2020, May 31). Anger floods cities across the U.S.; Pentagon could order military police to Minneapolis, report says. *USA Today*. Medium.com/@BarackObama/ how-to-make-this-moment-the-turning-point-for-real-change

4 Arenge, A., Perry, S., & Dartunorro, C. (2018, May 29). *Poll: 64 percent of Americans say racism remains a major problem*. NBC News.

5 Horowitz, J. M., Brown, A., & Cox, K. (2019, April 9). *Race in America*. Pew Research Center. www.pewsocialtrends. org/2019/04/09/race-in-america-2019

6 Federal Bureau of Investigation. (2018). *About hate crime statistcs, 2018*. ucr.fbi.gov/hate-crime/2018/; *New York Times*. (2019, November 12). Hate crime violence hits 16 year high, FBI reports. www.nytimes.com/2019/11/12/us/hate-crimes-fbi

7 Fingerhut, H. (2019, July 16). *Polls show sour view of race relations in Trump's America*. Associated Press. apnews.com/277/fe31

8 Voytko, L. (2020, January 17). 8 in 10 Black Americans view Trump as "a racist," poll finds. *Forbes*. www.forbes.com.sites. lisettervoytko

Introduction

1 Anapol, A. (March 29, 2019). Associated Press offers new guidelines to media on 'racially charged' vs 'racist'. *The Hill*. Retrieved from

www.thehill.com/homenews/436507-ap-offers-new-guidelines-to-media-on-racially-charged-vs-racist

2   Arenge, A., Perry, S., & Dartunorro, C. (May 29, 2018). *Poll: 64 percent of Americans say racism remains a majorproblem.* NBC News.

3   CNN.com (Aug 18, 2017). Retrieved 12/1/2019 from www.cnn.com.politics.blacks-white-racism-united-states

4   Associated Press, April 15, 2014.

5   Greenwald, A.G., & Krieger, L.H. (2006). Implicit bias: Scientific foundations. *California Law Review*, 94 (4). 945–967.6. Southern Poverty Law Center (2018). Hate map. Retrieved 12/1/2019 from Splcenter.org/hate-map.

6   Ibid.

7   Maxouris, C.. (May 27, 2020). George Floyd's family says four officers involved in his death should be charged with murder. Retrieved from msn.com/en-us/news/us/George-floyds-family-says-four-officers-involved-in-his-death-should-be-charged-with-murder.

8   Pilkington, E. (April 25, 2020). Will justice finally be done for Emmett Till? *The Guardian.* Retrieved from www.theguardian.com.us.news.apr.emmett-till.

9   Noah, T. (2019). *Born a crime.* New York, NY: Penguin Random House.

10 *Washington Post* (Sept 3, 2019). Mississippi wedding. Retrieved 12/1/2019 from www.washingtonpost.com.nation.2019/9/3.mississippi-wedding

11 MSN News, Aug 24, 2013

12 Ibid.

13 Bulosan, C. (1973). *America is in the heart.* Seattle, WA: University of Washington Press.

14 Southern Poverty Law Center, op cit.

15 *New York Times* editorial board (July 19, 2019). The real meaning of 'Send Her Back'. Retrieved 12/1/2019 from NYTimes.com/2019.07/18/opinion/trump-rally-send-her-back-html.

Chapter 1

1   Dulin-Keita, A., Hannon, L., Fernandez, J. R., & Cockerham, W. C. (2011). The defining moment: Children's conceptualization of race and experience with racial discrimination. *Ethnic Racial Studies*, 34(4), 662–682.

2   Ibid.

3   Noah, T. (2016). *Born a crime*. Random House.

4   Bonham, V., Warshauer-Baker, E., & Collins, F. S. (2005). Race and ethnicity in the genome era: The complexity of constructs. *American Psychologist, 60*(1), 9–15.

5   Simpson, G. E., & Yinger, J. M. (1985). *Racial and cultural minorities: An analysis of prejudice and discrimination*. Plenum.

6   Darwin, C. (1859). *On the origin of species. Or the preservation of favored races in the struggle for life*. Down, Bromley, Kent.

7   Boyd, R., & Silk, J. B. (2018). *How humans evolved*. Norton.

8   Graves, J. L. (2010). Biological v. social definitions of race: Implications for modern biomedical research. *The Review of Black Political Economy, 37*(1), 43–60; Jorde, I., & Wooding, S. (2004). Genetic variation, classification and "race." *Nature Genetics, 36*, 528–533.

9   Jorde & Wooding (2004).

10 Serre, D., & Paabo, S. (2004). Evidence for gradients of human diversity within and among continents. *Genome Research, 14*(9), 1679–1685.

11 Bashford, A., & Levine, P. (Eds.). (2010). *The Oxford handbook of the history of eugenics*. Oxford University Press.

12 Ibid.

13 Saini, A. (2019). *Superior: The return of race science*. Beacon Press.

14 Bashford & Levine (2010).

15 Ibid.

16 Ibid.

17 Ibid.

18 Saini (2019).

19 U.S. Census Bureau (2017).

20 Ibid.

21 Jones, J. M. (1997). *Prejudice and racism* (2nd ed.). McGraw-Hill.

22 Ibid.

23 Bashford & Levine (2010).

24 Allport, G. W. (1954). *The nature of prejudice*. Addison-Wesley.

25 Pew Research Center. (2013, August 22).

26 Associated Press. (2012).

27 Cole, D. (2009). *No equal justice: Race and class in the American criminal justice system*. The New Press.

28 Ibid.

29 Eberhardt, J., Davies, P. G., Purdie-Vaughn, V. J., & Johnson, S. I. (2006). Looking deathworthy: Perceived stereotypes of Black defendants predict capital sentencing outcomes. *Psychological Science*, *17*(5), 383–386.

30 *USA Today*. (2019, November 6). "I was appalled": Black customers recount alleged racist request at Buffalo Wild Wings near Chicago.

31 NBC News. (2013, October 24). *Black teen arrested after buying $350 designer belt.*

32 Tan, A. (2020). *Communication and prejudice: Theories, effects and consequences* (3rd ed.). Cognella.

33 Associated Press (2012).

34 Sides, J., & Gross, K. (2013). Stereotypes of Muslims and support for the war on terror. *Journal of Politics*, *75*(3), 583–598.

35 Greenwald, A. G., & Krieger, L. H. (2006). Implicit bias: Scientific foundations. *California Law Review*, *94*(4), 945–967.

36 Greenwald, A. G., Nosek, B. A., & Banaji, M. R. (2003). Understanding and using the Implicit Association Test: An improved scoring algorithm. *Journal of Personality and Social Psychology*, *85*(2), 197–216; Eberhardt, J. (2019). *Biased*. Random House.

37 Noah (2019); Omond, R. (1986). *The apartheid handbook* (2nd ed.). Penguin.

38 Omond (1986).

39 Eberhardt (2019).

40 Eberhardt (2019); Tan (2020).

41 Ibid.

42 Eberhardt et al. (2006).

43 Federal Glass Ceiling Commission. (1995). *Solid investments: Making full use of the nation's human capital*. U.S. Department of Labor.

44 Li, E. P., Min H. J., Belk, R. W., Kimura, J., & Bahl, S. (2008). Skin lightening and beauty in four Asian cultures. *Advances in Consumer Research*, *35*, 444–449.

45 Frith, K., Cheng, H., & Shaw, P. (2004). Race and beauty: A comparison of Asian and Western models in women's magazine advertisements. *Sex Roles*, *50*(1), 53–61.

46 Bashford & Levine (2010); Painter, N. (2011). *The history of White people*. Norton.

47 Tan (2020).

Chapter 2

1 Fiske, S. T. (2000). Stereotyping, prejudice, and discrimination at the seam between the centuries: Evolution, culture, mind, and brain. *European Journal of Social Psychology, 30*(3), 299–322.

2 Kelly, D., Quinn, P., Slater, A., Lee, K., Gibson, A., Smith, M., Ge, L., & Pascalis, O. (2005). Three-month-olds, but not newborns, prefer own-race faces. *Developmental Science, 8*(6), 31–36.

3 Ibid.

4 Ibid.

5 Lee, K., Quinn, D., & Pascalis, O. (2017). Face race processing and racial bias in early development: A perceptual-social linkage. *Current Directions in Psychological Science, 26*(3), 256–262.

6 Ibid.

7 Kelly et al. (2005).

8 Winkler, E. N. (2009). Children are not colorblind: How young children learn race. *PACE: Practical Approaches for Continuing Education, 3*(3), 1–8; Katz, P. A., & Kofkin, J. A. (1997). Race, gender, and young children. In S. S. Luthar & J. A. Burack (Eds.) *Developmental psychopathology: Perspectives on adjustment, risk and disorder* (pp. 51–74). Cambridge University Press.

9 Sinclair, S., Dunn, E., & Lowery, B. (2005). The relationship between parental racial attitudes and children's implicit prejudice. *Journal of Experimental Social Psychology, 41*(3), 283–289.

10 Ibid.

11 Tan, A. (2020). *Communication and prejudice: Theories, effects and interventions* (3rd ed.). Cognella.

12 Ibid.

13 Ibid.

14 Ibid.

15 Ibid.

16 Barreto, M., Manzano, S., & Segura, G. (2012). *The impact of media stereotypes on opinions and attitudes towards Latinos.* National Hispanic Media Coalition. www.nhmc.org

17 Tan (2020).

18 Shaheen, J. (2008). *Guilty: Hollywood's verdict on Arabs after 9/11.* Olive Branch Press.

19 Ibid.

20 Hodson, G., & Busseri, M. A. (2012). Bright minds and dark attitudes: Lower cognitive ability predicts greater prejudice through

right-wing ideology and low intergroup contact. *Psychological Science*, 23(2), 187–185.

21 Ibid.

22 Ibid.

23 Schafer, J. A., & Mulins, C. W. (2014). Awakenings: The emergence of White supremacist ideologies. *Deviant Behavior*, 35(3), 173–196.

24 Stephan, W. G., & Stephan, C. W. (2000). An integrated theory of prejudice. In S. Oskamp (Ed.), *Reducing prejudice and discrimination* (pp. 23–46). Lawrence Erlbaum.

25 Stephan, W. G., Ybarra, O., & Bachman, G. (2001). Prejudice toward immigrants. *Journal of Applied Social Psychology*, 29(11), 2221–2237.

26 Ibid.

Chapter 3

1 Faucet, R. (2020, June 21). What we know about the shooting death of Ahmaud Arbery. *New York Times*. www.nyTimes.com/article'ahmaud-arbery-shooting-georgia.html

2 Anti-Defamation League. (2015, July). *With hate in their hearts. The state of White supremacy in the U.S.* www.adl.org/education/resources/reports/state-of-white-supremacy

3 Greenwald, A. G., & Krieger, L. H. (2006). Implicit bias: Scientific foundations. *California Law Review*, 94(4), 945–967.

4 Tsesis, A. (2009). The regulation of hate speech in a democracy. *Wake Forest Law Review*, 44, 497–502.

5 Ibid.

6 Bojarska, K. (2019). *The dynamics of hate speech and counter speech in the social media: Summary of scientific research.* Centre for Internet and Human Rights. Cihr.eu/wp-content/uploads/2018/10/the-dynamics-of-hate-speech-and-counter-speech-in-the-social-media_English-1.pdf

7 Anti-Defamation League Center. (2019). Defining extremism: A glossary of White supremacist terms, movements and philosophies. www.adl.org.what-we-do>combat-hate>extremism-terrorism-bigotry

8 Southern Poverty Law Center. (2019). *Hate map.* http://www.splcenter.org/get-informed/hate-map; Woodyard, C. (2019, February 20). Hate group count hits 20-year high amid rise in White supremacy, report says. *USA Today*. https://www.usatoday.com/

story/news/nation/2019/02/20/hate-groups-white-power-suprem-acists-southern-povertry-law-center/2918416002/

9 Federal Bureau of Investigation. (2019). *Hate crime data collection guidelines.* https://www.fbi.gov/ucr/guidelines

10 Anti-Defamation League, 2019.

11 Ibid.

12 Southern Poverty Law Center, 2019.

13 Gardner, K. (2018). *Social media: Where voices of hate find a place to preach.* News21. https://hateinamerica.news21.com/

14 Ibid.

15 Anti-Defamation League, 2019

16 Ibid.

17 Ibid.

18 Ibid.

19 Gardner, 2018.

20 Anti-Defamation League, 2019.

21 Gardner, 2018.

22 Forscher, P., & Kelly, N. (2017). A psychological profile of the alt-right. *Perspectives on Psychological Science.* https://doi.org/10.31234/osf.io/c9uvw

23 Akhtar, A. (2019, August 10). Psychologists break down the insecurities that fuel White supremacists. *Business Insider.*; Kruglanski, A., Jasko, K., & Webber, D. (2008). The making of violent extremists. *Review of General Psychology,* 22(1), 107–120. https://doi.org/10.1037/gpr0000144

24 Forscher & Kelly, 2017. Also Kruglanski et al., 2008.

25 Anti-Defamation League, 2015.

26 Neville, H., Roderick, L., Duran, G., Lee, R., & Browne, L. (2002). Construction and initial validation of the Color-Blind Racial Attitudes Scale (CoBras). *Journal of Counseling Psychology,* 47(1), 59–70.

27 McConahay, J. B. (1986). Modern racism, ambivalence, and the Modern Racism Scale. In J. Dovidio & S. Gaertner (Eds.), *Prejudice, discrimination and racism* (pp. 91–125). Academic Press.

28 Ibid.

29 Bogardus, E. S. (1933). A social distance scale. *Sociology & Social Research,* 17, 265–271; Karakayali, N. (2009). Social distance and affective orientations. *Sociological Forum,* 24(3), 538–562.

30 Greenwald, A. G., & Krieger, L. H. (2006). Implicit bias: Scientific foundations. *California Law Review,* 94(4), 945–967.

31 Ibid.

32 Ibid.

33 Greenwald, A. G., Poehlman, T. A., Uhlmann, E. I., & Banaji, M. R. (2009). Understanding and using the Implicit Association Test: Meta-analysis of predictive validity. *Journal of Personality and Social Psychology*, 97(1), 17–41.

34 Mineo, L. (2020, June 4). Orlando Patterson explains why America can't escape its racist roots. *Harvard Gazette*. news.harvard.edu/gazette/story/3030/orlando-patterson-explains-why-America-can't-escape-its-racist-roots/

Chapter 4

1 Pager, D., & Shepherd, H. (2008). The sociology of discrimination: Racial discrimination in employment, housing, credit and consumer markets. *Annual Review of Sociology*, 34, 181–209; Pittman, C. (2020). "Shopping while Black": Black consumers' management of racial stigma and racial profiling in retail settings. *Journal of Consumer Culture*, 20(1), 3–22.

2 Tan, A. (2020). *Communication and prejudice: Theories, effects and interventions* (3rd ed.). Cognella.

3 *Huffington Post*. (2018, December 14); *Vox*. (2018, December 31); *Independent*. (2018, May 7); *U.S. News*. (2019, September 9).

4 *Huffington Post* (2018).

5 NBC News. (2013, October 24). *Black teen arrested after buying $350 designer belt*.

6 Pittman (2020).

7 Ibid.

8 Ibid.

9 Stanford University. (2019). *The Stanford Open Policing Project*. Openpolicing.stanford.edu

10 Ibid.

11 *The Spokesman Review*. (2020, January 2). WSP stops Native drivers more, finds less.

12 Ibid.

13 Tan (2020); Bielen, S., Marneffe, W., & Mocan, N. (2020, May). *Racial bias and in-group bias in judicial decisions: Evidence from virtual reality courtrooms*. National Bureau of Economic Research (Working paper no. 25355).

14 Ibid.

15 Ibid.

16 Ibid.

17 Levinson, J. D., Cai, H., & Young, D. (2010). Guilty by implicit racial bias: The guilty/not guilty Implicit Association Test. *Ohio State Journal of Criminal Law, 8*(1), 187–208.

18 Oliver, M. B., & Fonash, D. (2002). Race and crime in the news: Whites' identification and misidentification of violent and nonviolent and nonviolent criminal suspects. *Media Psychology, 4*(2), 137–156.

19 Levinson et al. (2010).

20 Correll, J., Hudson, S. M., Guillermo, S., & Ma, D. (2014). The police officer's dilemma: A decade of research on racial bias in the decision to shoot. *Social and Personality Psychology Compass, 8*(5), 201–213.

21 Eller, B. (2017). The behavioral dynamics of shooter bias in virtual reality: The role of race, armed status, and distance on threat perception and shooting dynamics [Doctoral dissertation, University of Cincinnati].

22 Weir, K. (2016). Racial disparities in law enforcement. *Psychological Science, 47*(11), 36.

23 Correll, J., Park, B., Judd, C., & Wittenbrink, B. (2007). The influence of stereotypes on decisions to shoot. *European Journal of Social Psychology, 37*(6), 1102–1117.

24 Ibid.

25 Spencer, K. B., Charbonneau, A., & Glasser, J. (2016). Implicit bias and policing. *Social and Personality Psychology Compass, 10*(1), 50–63.

26 Ibid.

27 Correll et al. (2007).

28 O'Carroll, E. (2019, September 11). When keepers of the peace harbor hate. *The Christian Science Monitor.* www.Csmonitor.com/USA/Justice/2019/0911/When-keepers-of-the-peace-harbor-hate

29 Hall, A. V., Hall, E. V., & Perry, J. L. (2016). Black and blue. Exploring racial bias and law enforcement in the killings of unarmed black male civilians. *American Psychologist, 7*(3), 175–186.

30 Spencer et al. (2016).

31 O'Carroll (2019).

32 De Angelis, T. (2019, March). How does implicit bias by physicians affect patients' health care? *American Psychological Association, 50*(3), 22.

33 Dovidio, J., Eggly, S., Albrecht, T., Hagiwara, N., & Penner, C. (2016). Racial biases in medicine and healthcare disparities. *Testing Psychometrics, Methodology in Applied Psychology, 23*(4), 489–510.

34 Ibid.

35 Chisolm-Straker, M., & Straker, H. O. (2017). Implicit bias in U.S. medicine: Complex findings and incomplete conclusions. *International Journal of Human Rights in Healthcare, 10*(1), 43–55.

36 De Angelis (2019).

37 Ibid.

38 Green, A. R., Carney, D. R., Pallin, D. J., Ngo, L. H., Raymond, K. L., Iezzoni, I. I., & Banaji, M. R. (2007). Implicit bias among physicians and its prediction of thrombolysis decisions for Black and White patients. *Journal of General Internal Medicine, 22*(9), 1231–1238.

39 Ibid.

40 De Angelis (2019).

41 Weir, K. (2016, November). Inequality at school. *American Psychological Association, 47*(10), 42–45; U.S. Department of Education, Office of Civil Rights. (2016, June). 2013–2014 civil rights data collection: Key data highlights in equity and opportunity gaps in our nation's public schools. http://www2.ed.gov/about/offices/list/ocr/docs/crdc-2013-14.html

42 Gilliam, W. S., Maupin, A. N., Reyes, C. R., Accavitti, B. S., & Shic, F. (2016, September 28). *Do early educators' implicit biases regarding sex and race relate to behavior expectations and recommendations for preschool expulsions and suspensions?* Yale University Child Study Center, 2–18.

43 Ibid.

44 Ibid.

45 Weir (2016).

46 Ibid.

47 Dee, T., & Gershenson, S. (2017). Unconscious bias in the classroom: Evidence and opportunities. Google. https://goo.gl/06Btqi

48 Ibid.

49 Ibid.

50 Ibid.

51 Tan, A. (2018). *Communication and prejudice: Theories, effects and interventions.* Cognella.

52 Dee & Gershenson (2017).

53 Anderson, J. (2019, November 20). *Harvard EdCast: Unconscious bias in schools*. Harvard Graduate School of Education. https:// www.facebook.com/HarvardEducation

54 Ibid.

55 Ibid

56 Warikoo, N., Sinclair, S., Fei, J., & Jacoby-Senghor, D. (2016). Examining racial bias in education: A new approach. *Educational Researcher, 45*(9), 508–514.

57 Ibid.

58 Ibid.

59 Ibid.

60 Ibid.

61 Parks, G. S., & Heard, D. C. (2009). *"Assassinate the nigger ape": Obama, implicit imagery, and the dire consequences of racist jokes.* Cornell Law Faculty (Working paper 61). http://scholarship. law,cornell.edu/clsops_paper 61

62 Ibid.

63 Ibid.

64 Ibid.

65 Ibid.

66 Ibid

67 Ibid.

68 Pettigrew, T. F. (2017). Social psychological perspectives on Trump supporters. *Journal of Social and Political Psychology, 5*(1), 107–116.

69 Hooghe, M., & Dassonneville, R. (2018, July). Explaining the Trump vote: The effect of racist resentment and anti-immigrant sentiments. *PS: Political Science and Politics, 51*(3), 528–534.

70 Ibid.

71 Pettigrew (2017); also Schaffner, B. F. (2018). *Follow the racist? The consequences of Trump's expressions of prejudice for mass rhetoric.* Semantic Scholar. semanticscholar.org/paper/Follow-the-Racist-the-consequences-of-Trump-'s-of-Schaffner/; Schaffner, B. F., MacWilliams, M., & Nteta, T. (2018). Understanding White polarization in the 2016 vote for president: The sobering role of racism and sexism. *Political Science Quarterly, 134*(1), 9–34.

72 Luttig, M. D., Federico, C. M., & Lavine, H. (2017). Supporters and opponents of Donald Trump respond differently to racial cues: An experimental analysis. *Research and Politics, 4*(4).

73 Ibid.

74 Greenwald, A. G., Smith, C. T., Sriram, N., Bar-Anan, Y., & Nosek, B. (2009). Race attitude measures predicted vote in the 2008 U.S. presidential election. *Analysis of Social Issues and Public Policy, 9*(1), 241–253.

75 Knowles, E., & Schaumberg, R. (2010). Racial prejudice predicts opposition to Obama and his health care reform plan. *Journal of Experimental Social Psychology, 46*(2), 420–423.

76 Tan, A. (2020). *Communication and prejudice: Theories, effects and interventions* (3rd ed.). Cognella.

77 Bertrand, M., & Mullainathan, S. (2004). Are Emily and Greg more employable than Lakisha and Jamal? A field experiment on labor market discrimination. *The American Economic Review, 94*(4), 991–1013.

78 Rooth, D. (2010). Automatic associations and discrimination in hiring: Real world evidence. *Labour Economics, 17*(3), 523–534.

79 McConnell, A. R., & Leibold, J. M. (2001). Relations among the Implicit Association Test, discriminatory behaviors, and explicit measures of racial attitudes. *Journal of Experimental Social Psychology, 37*(5), 435–442.

80 Gawronski, B., Geschke, D., & Banse, R. (2003). Explicit bias in impression formation: Associations influence the construal of individuating information. *European Journal of Social Psychology, 33*(5), 573–589.

81 Ibid.

82 Ellerbeck, A. (2020, April 18). *Over 30 percent of Americans have witnessed COVID-19 bias against Asians, poll says*. NBC News. www.nbcnews.com/news/Asian-america/over-30-americans-have-witnessed; Peng, S., & Co, E. (2020, April 4). *Smashed windows and racist graffiti: Vandals target Asian Americans*. NBC News. www.msn.com/en-us/news/us/smahed-windows-and-racist-graffiti-target-asian-americans

83 Haynes, S. (March 6, 2020). As Coronavirus spreads, so does xenophobia and anti-Asian racism. *Time.* www.msn.com/en-us/news/world/as-coronovirus-spreads-so-does-xenophobia-and-anti-asian-racism/

84 Ibid.

85 Zhou, L. (April 4, 2020). *How Coronavirus is surfacing America's deep-seated anti-Asian biases*. Vax. www.msn.com/en-us/news/us/how-the-coronavirus-is

86 O'Donnell & Associates. (2020, April 17). *Corona big book main messages*; NBC News. (2020, April 28).

87 Ibid.

88 Flatley, D., & Wingrove, J. (May 2, 2020). Trump seeks to pin blame on China, yet reprisal is uncertain. *Bloomberg News*. www.msn.com.en-us?politics/trump-seeks-to-pin-blame-on-China-yet-reprisal-is-uncertain

89 Ibid.

90 Steele, C. M. (2010). *Whistling Vivaldi and other clues in how stereotypes affect us*. Norton.

91 Steele, C. M. (1999). Thin ice: "Stereotype threat" and Black college students. *The Atlantic*, 44–54.

92 Ibid.

Chapter 5

1 Nosek, B. A., Greenwald, A. G., & Banaji, M. R. (2007). The Implicit Association Test at age 7: A methodological and conceptual review. In J. A. Bargh (Ed.), *Automatic processes in social thinking and behavior* (pp. 265–292). Psychology Press.

2 Paluck, E. L., & Green, D. P. (2009). Prejudice reduction: What works? A review and assessment of research and practice. *Annual Review of Psychology, 60*, 339–367.

3 Ibid.

4 Devine, P. G., Forscher, P. S., Austin, A. J., & Cox, W. (2012). Long-term reduction in implicit bias: A prejudice habit-breaking intervention. *Journal of Experimental Social Psychology, 48*(6), 1267–1278.

5 Ibid.

6 Legault, L., Gutsell, J., & Inzlicht, M. (2011). Ironic effects of antiprejudice messages: How motivational interventions can reduce (but also increase) prejudice. *Psychological Science, 22*(12), 1472–1477.

7 Moskowitz, G., & Li, P. (2011). Egalitarian goals trigger stereotype inhibition: A proactive form of stereotype control. *Journal of Experimental Social Psychology, 47*(1), 103–116.

8 Vescio, T. K., Sechrist, G. B., & Paolucci, M. P. (2003). Perspective taking and prejudice reduction: The mediational role of empathy around situational attributions. *European Journal of Social Psychology, 33*(4), 455–472; Finlay, K., & Stephan, W.

(2000). Improving intergroup relations. The effects of empathy on racial attitudes. *Journal of Applied Social Psychology, 30*(8), 1720–1737.

9 Ball-Rokeach, S., Rokeach, M., & Grube, J. (1984). *The great American values test.* The Free Press.

10 Pettigrew, T. F., & Tropp, L. R. (2006). A meta-analytic test of intergroup contact theory. *Journal of Personality and Social Psychology, 90*(5), 751–783.

11 Associated Press. (2013, September 5).

12 Turner, R., Crisp, R., & Lambert, E. (2007). Imagining intergroup contact can improve intergroup attitudes. *Group Processes and Intergroup Relations, 10*(10), 427–441.

13 Turner, R., & Crisp, R. (2010). Imagining intergroup contact reduces implicit prejudice. *British Journal of Social Psychology, 49*(1), 129–142.

14 Ibid.

15 Tan, A. (2020). *Communication and prejudice: Theories, effects and interventions* (3rd ed.). Cognella.

16 Ibid.

17 Richeson, J. A., & Nussbaum, R. J. (2004). The impact of multiculturalism versus colorblindness on racial bias. *Journal of Experimental Social Psychology, 40*(3), 417–423.

18 Dasgupta, N., & Greenwald, A. G. (2001). On the malleability of automatic attitudes. Combating automatic prejudice with images of admired and disliked individuals. *Journal of Personality and Social Psychology, 81*(5), 800–814.

19 Associated Press Style Book, 2013. https://www.apstylebook. com/

20 Asian American Journalists Association (2000). *ALL-AMERICAN: How to cover Asian America.* www.aaja.org/ aajahandbookupdate/

21 Tan (2020).

22 Ibid.

Made in the USA
Monee, IL
21 January 2021